D1403393

Family-Institution Interaction

PETER LANG
New York • Washington, D.C./Baltimore • Bern
Frankfurt am Main • Berlin • Brussels • Vienna • Oxford

Cynthia Wallat

Family-Institution Interaction

New Refrains

PETER LANG
New York • Washington, D.C./Baltimore • Bern
Frankfurt am Main • Berlin • Brussels • Vienna • Oxford

Library of Congress Cataloging-in-Publication Data

Wallat, Cynthia.
Family-institution interaction: new refrains / Cynthia Wallat.
p. cm.
Includes bibliographical references and index.
1. Parent and child. 2. Communication in the family.
3. Family. 4. Child development. I. Title.
HQ755.85 .W35   306.874—dc21   2001050664
ISBN 0-8204-5830-9

Die Deutsche Bibliothek-CIP-Einheitsaufnahme

Wallat, Cynthia:
Family-institution interaction: new refrains / Cynthia Wallat.
—New York; Washington, D.C./Baltimore; Bern;
Frankfurt am Main; Berlin; Brussels; Vienna; Oxford: Lang.
ISBN 0-8204-5830-9

Cover design by Joni Holst

The paper in this book meets the guidelines for permanence and durability
of the Committee on Production Guidelines for Book Longevity
of the Council of Library Resources.

Printed in the United States of America

Contents

Illustration

Tables

Preface

One hallmark of social science since the early part of the twentieth century is to discover how parts of a social system such as families and other institutions fit together, the accounts of such being marked as a promising direction for the acquisition of knowledge of social phenomena including family-institution interaction. The scope of the social sciences has included attention to the policy themes of involving family members in identifying what is required for optimizing children's chances for educational success, physical health, and social competence, and maximizing family members' participation in the structure and organization of activities contributing to human development. In spite of such sustained attention to recognizing families as important human development systems, a growing number of family policy groups assert that programs such as Head Start could be better.

The year 2000 marked Head Start's thirty-fifth year of trying to reach the ideal of doing better at defining quality in terms of the nature of children's progression and transition within and across family and public institutional contexts rather than limiting the search for quality to cognitive properties that define the nature of children's later school achievement. Supporters continue to expect policies of child care and development to meet the legislative intent of preparedness for school—or even preschool—and thereby demonstrate responsiveness to continuing testing and assessment issues. However, though acknowledging that measuring individual children's cognitive behaviors has become the norm for measuring progress, many researchers have identified additional purposes—and laid much of the groundwork—for defining progress while including all participants in upbringing.

The intent of this research monograph is to contribute to constructing a response to the challenge of underachievement and the widespread belief that Head Start and model state prekindergarten programs could be better. Members of task force groups created by the Carnegie Corporation of New York articulate the problem of underachievement in the following way:

"Underachievement is not a crisis of certain groups: it is not limited to the poor; it is not a problem affecting *other* people's children. Many middle— and upper—income children are also falling behind" (Carnegie Corporation of New York 1996, p. viii).

Descriptions are presented in the chapters that follow of a decade of efforts in assessing cognitive and social behaviors associated with long-term success of infant, toddlers', and preschoolers' learning and development. These descriptions are followed by a set of suggestions from the same time period for developing new ways to think about the interaction of upbringing functions across family and public institutions. A collection of lessons learned about language and interaction from studies across family and public organizational settings is then presented as a strategy for drawing these areas of study together, thereby providing a base for practitioners, researchers, family members, and policymakers to help articulate whether standards developed for Head Start programs and model state prekindergarten programs by professional associations are being accomplished.

Acknowledgments

The start of this venture in thinking about what we know about how a child becomes a member of society began at the University of Pittsburgh when I took my first graduate course in early childhood with Professor Denis Donegan in 1971. He asked the class to read through a list of topics and choose one that we were interested in exploring under his guidance. At our first meeting on choosing a topic Dr. Donegan told me I would sustain my curiosity about childhood and society by asking myself: What do we know, and why don't we know more? Three years later the topic I chose became my first publication: *A Comparative Analysis of Early Childhood Education Objectives in the United States, the Soviet Union, and England.* By 1975 I completed my doctoral studies after having the opportunity to acquire a program of study using every part of the university because Dr. Donegan believed that would ensure that I had an ecological perspective on upbringing for all subsequent studies I would undertake to answer my question: How does a child becomes a member of society?

I dedicate this research monograph to Denis Donegan for helping me frame my research career, to Lois-ellin Datta for supporting my continuing curiosity about children and the variations surrounding their lives, and her continuing commitment to demonstrating how inquiry can indeed connect developmental research and public policy, and to Irving Lazar for guiding me through my tenure as a federal research and development project officer as well as my academic career. In addition, Mark Riordan, from the vantage point of an academic discipline that believes that good writing can sometimes be found, has given support through his willingness to help nudge me away from academese by being interested in what I was trying to write and having wonderful conversations that always created the feeling that the ideas expressed in this monograph were worth trying to express. Finally, and most importantly, I am grateful to Geoff for the gift of being able to be a part in his becoming a member of society.

CHAPTER ONE

Introduction

S ince the inception of Head Start in 1965, the federal government has
funded preschool programs for millions of young children and their
families. That the twentieth century $30 billion taxpayer investment
has succeeded in preparing more than 15 million participating children for
school is without question and needs no further empirical support. The
mood of policy analysts contemplating this success and family researchers
interested in adding a meaningful new generation of research methods,
however, is more accurately captured in news headlines such as "Head Start
Works, But It Could Be Better" (Jacobson 1999).

Policymakers in Washington oftentimes reward success, especially in
social service delivery, by expanding the agency's mission. Sometimes the
expansion, though logical, pushes the agency into completely new areas,
where measuring, and therefore ensuring, program success means developing entirely new assessment models.

As policymakers contemplate the content of evaluations in terms of the
consequences of adding "from welfare to work" programming for the parents of children participating in Head Start, they are faced with the daunt-
ing task of moving beyond simply assessing the cognitive abilities and social
preparedness of a child. Now the focus turns to quantifying interaction
among the participants as a family and their interaction with the agencies
responsible for preparing them.

A variety of studies and evaluations conducted since the first summer of
Head Start's operation have attempted to answer policy and practice questions based on the program's legislated intent. These studies were conducted based on the underlying assumption that realizing the benefit of
public money dollars to society requires new forms of integration of insti-

tutions, especially to accomplish linkages between families and other institutions. The first set of linkages would give a boost to children's social and
academic development. More recently, the goal of linkages of interaction
structures across institutions is to include families with infants and toddlers
and to help parents on welfare to move to work (Parker, Piotrkowski,
Kesslar-Sklar, Baker, Peay & Clark 1997).

The continued inclusion of evaluation requirements of Head Start
efforts since summer 1965 advances the claim that social science research
has the capacity to build upon its methods of social inquiry to study the
outcome of this new form of integration of the family as an institution and
Head Start as an institution. Quantitative researchers would be able to
develop explanations based on asking whether, and to what extent, variance in adults' interactions with children causes variance in children's social
and academic development.

Analysis of data collected on adults dealing with problem behaviors
such as being aggressive, disruptive, or withdrawn might show that there is
a correlation between a certain set of adult language functions during interaction and the development of children's social skills. Qualitative
researchers would be able to ask how family interaction plays a role in child
and family development, what is the process that connects family interaction and family-institution interaction, and what are the processes through
which adults across both institutions interpret interactions between family
members as well as interactions between family members and members of
social institutions. In other words, qualitative and quantitative methods
would be used to address established social inquiry questions such as: Why
is it that a given form, or structure, or social situation is associated with a
certain set of functions? What structures are required for the exercise of the
specified functions of this new form of family-institution interaction?
(Nagel 1961).

OVERVIEW

This research monograph identifies qualitative and quantitative methods that have been reported in the literature to address these questions. Recent developments such as the reauthorization of Head

Start, the continued rise in fiscal year budgets for accomplishing its traditional goals, and the expansion of research to develop accountability measures for Head Start Standards for infants, toddlers, and preschoolers provide new incentives for social science researchers to study family-institution interaction (Congressional Research Service 2001; U.S. Department of Health and Human Services 1998, 1999). For example, in addition to the identification of twenty-six parent interviews and five staff interviews as data sources for evaluating how each Head Start program meets the five performance standards (enhancing children's growth and development; strengthening families; providing services and/or linking children and families to services; and ensuring well-managed programs that involve parents in decision-making), a second set of descriptions of measures included in a nationwide study of Early Head Start includes descriptions of 12 staff interviews and over 80 interviews of 3,000 participating families living in a wide variety of locations across the United States.

The purpose of presenting reviews of a decade of child development studies of parent-child interaction is to provide readers with a set of indicators of what is known and unknown about communication as family members link with other institutional settings, thereby providing a base for reconsidering possibilities for approaching such required interviews in ways that will build new knowledge of family-institution interaction.

At issue is not the superiority of one approach over another, but how to situate empirical findings and theoretical directions within the normative policy goal of strengthening families through ensuring their participation in health and education services and thereby building a sense of community with program deliverers (Fischer 1998; Zimmerman 1999).

Table 1. Head Start Performance Standards Objectives, Indicators, and Data Sources [26 Parent Interviews]

Performance Standards Objective	Enhance Children's Growth and Development [Data Sources: Parent Interviews]	Strengthening Families [Data Sources: Parent Interviews]	Providing Services and/or Linking Children and Families to Educational, Health, and Nutrition Services [Data Sources: Parent Interviews]	Linking Children and Families to Needed Community Services [Data Sources: Parent Interviews]
Performance Indicator	Child's Growth (Change) in Emergence Literacy, Language Skills, Numerical Skills, General Cognitive Skills—Memory, Reasoning, Problem Solving [1 through 4]	Child's home safety; environment safety [9]	Parent's satisfaction with the helpfulness of Head Start Services and Support [16]	Parents receive needed social services (e.g., child care, housing services) [19]
	Child's Improved Positive Attitudes Towards Learning [5]	Child's home learning environment [10]	Parent's satisfaction with Head Start programs support and respect for children's cultures [17]	Parents receive needed educational services (e.g., GED classes) [20]
	Child's Task Mastery [6]	Parent's limit-setting and disciplinary methods [11]	Parent's satisfaction with meeting the special needs of their children with disabilities because of Head Start [18]	Parents help children make the transition from Head Start to kindergarten (e.g., talking to kindergarten teachers, visiting new school) [21]
	Child's Positive Social Behavior [7]	Parent's sense of control over their own lives (including parent's depression, social support network) [12]		Child and family members have on ongoing source of continuous, accessible health care [22]
	Child's Social Interaction with Peers [8]	Parent's receipt of needed employment, job training, education, literacy services [13 through 15]		Parents secured needed health services (e.g., child immunizations, mental health services) [23]
				Parents provided with linkages to child care [24]
				Parents have stable child care services [25]
				Parent influence program operations [26]

Table 2. Head Start Performance Standards Objectives, Indicators, and Data Sources [5 Staff Interviews]

Performance Objective	Providing Services and/or Linking Children and Families to Community [Data Sources: Staff Interviews]	Ensuring Well-Managed Programs that Involve Parents in Decision-Making [Data Sources: Staff Interviews]
Performance Indicator	Effectiveness of Head Start in helping parents receive needed educational services, helping children and parents make the transition from Head Start to kindergarten, helping link with health care services to obtain needed care for children and families [1]	Value/Importance of program goal regarding meeting parent needs [2] Effectiveness of program goal regarding providing appropriate ongoing training and staff development [3] Effectiveness of program goal regarding providing ongoing and effective staff development and training activities [4] The extent to which Head Start programs maintain a positive organizational climate that offers administrative and peer support and teamwork [5]

Source: The information presented in Table 1 and Table 2 is based on a review of content that was identified using the following search steps: (a) go to http:// www2 acf.dhhs.gov/programs/hsb/text_only_html/tablr_of_contents; (b) arrive at Head Start Program Performance Measures Progress Report—Table of Contents; (c) click on Appendix A—Performance Measures Matrix; (d) arrive at Appendix A: Head Start Program Goal, Objectives, Measures, Indicators and Data Sources (Note: This information was available on the Head Start Website in May 1999)

Table 3. Measures and Interviews Used in Early Head Start National Evaluation to Assess Contributions of Family Members to Infant and Toddler Development

Measures	81 Parent Interviews as Data Sources at
ASSESSMENT OBJECTIVE: PARENTING AND HOME ENVIRONMENT	
Knowledge of infant development	14 months
Knowledge of child health and development	24 months; 36 months
Parental distress and parent–child dysfunctional interaction	14 months; 24 months; 36 months
Parent values and beliefs—10 items selected from traditional authoritarian beliefs and progressive democratic beliefs subscales	24 months
Home environment reading and language activities	14 months; 24 months; 36 months
Parent activities to encourage language development, literacy, physical activities, and experiences of outside world	14 months; 24 months; 36 months
Parent beliefs about talking and reading to children	24 months
Ever separated overnight; number of separations; total time separated; where child stayed; and reasons for separations	14 months; 24 months; 36 months
Parental discipline—use of reasoning and developmental—appropriate approaches, incidence of spanking in previous week	14 months; 24 months; 36 months
Number of hours the television is on during a typical weekend day	14 months; 36 months
ASSESSMENT OBJECTIVE: PARENT'S CHARACTERISTICS	
Parent's depression, anxiety, alcohol abuse, and substance abuse	14 months; 24 months; 36 months
Parent's literacy	14 months

Continued on next page

Parent's language/cognition	24 months
Parent's health	14 months
Biological father's age at child's birth; father's current economic activity; father's educational level	14 months; 24 months
Biological father's age at child's birth; father's current economic activity; father's educational level—new father figure	36 months
Biological father's involvement with pregnancy and birth—when biological father was informed of the pregnancy; whether father was present at birth; whether father visited the baby in the hospital; whether the father discussed the pregnancy with the mother, attended prenatal doctor visits, or attended childbirth classes	14 months
Biological father helps mother care for child on a typical day—whether mother has had contact with nonresident biological father since child's first birthday; degree of conflict about where the child lives and how child is raised; how mother and father spend money on child; father visits; child support payments	24 months
Contact with father (e.g., lives with child and/or in household with mother and child); how long father has lived with mother since child's second birthday; whether father has had any contact with child since child's second birthday; how often father has seen child in previous three months; how often father has looked after child while mother did other things in past month	36 months
Nonresidental father's support for child—how often father has helped buy toys, clothes, or presents for child, paid for medical insurance or care, or given the mother extra money to help out; whether the mother has a new legal, an informal, or no child support agreement and date of new agreement; monthly amount father is supposed to pay and number of times father has paid under formal agreement	24 months; 36 months
Current relationship between mother and father—extent of contact; degree of conflict about where the child lives and how child is raised; how mother and father spend money on child; father visits; child support payments	14 months; 36 months

Continued on next page

Contact between child and father	14 months; 24 months; 36 months
Child's activities with father (reading, feeding, eating a meal, going outside, playing at home)	14 months; 24 months
Presence of and activities of a mother figure (i.e., mother figures may be important adults in some cultures, important mediator)	24 months

ASSESSMENT OBJECTIVE:
FAMILY FUNCTIONING

Number of adults and children in the family and their relationship to the focus child	14 months; 24 months; 36 months
Presence of mother's spouse or partner	24 months
Family routines around the child's bedtime (routine adherence and routine endorsement)	14 months
Family routines surrounding child's bedtime and TV viewing (routine adherence)	24 months
Family conflict	14 months; 24 months
Stressful life events	14 months; 24 months; 36 months
Social support	14 months
Proximity of family members and sources of social support	14 months

ASSESSMENT OBJECTIVE:
CHILD CARE USE

Type of child care currently used (age of current caregiver, age child began current child-care arrangement, length of time in nonparental child care per week, cost of current nonrelative provider)	14 months; 24 months; 36 months
Parent's relationship with current nonrelative provider	14 months; 24 months; 36 months

ASSESSMENT OBJECTIVE:
CHILD'S SOCIOEMOTIONAL
FUNCTIONING

Temperament (sociability, emotionality)	14 months

Continued on next page

Orientation towards parent; engagement   24 months
orientation towards examiner

Emotional regulation   24 months

Behavioral problems   24 months; 36 months

Child compliance with mother and   24 months
self-regulation during a challenging/
frustrating situation

Toddler attachment behaviors, including   24 months
social referencing, proximity and help-seeking,
and affective expressiveness

ASSESSMENT OBJECTIVE:
CHILD'S COGNITIVE AND
LANGUAGE DEVELOPMENT

Receptive Language   14 months

Expressive Language   24 months; *Note: At 36 months the data sources
                                              for Measures of child-care quality switch to
                                              Interviewer Observations of child-care setting,
                                              child-care provider, and focus child*

ASSESSMENT OBJECTIVE:
CHILD'S PHYSICAL HEALTH

National Health Interview Study (NHIS)   14 months; 24 months

Hospitalizations: Selected items from the   14 months; 24 months; 36 months
National Health Interview: hospitalizations
for accidents, injuries, jaundice, dehydration,
and pneumonia

Number of well-child visits   24 months

Use of safety precautions: Precautions to   14 months; 24 months; 36 months
reduce risk of accidents and unintentional
injury

Child's Heath Today: Sleeping, respiratory   14 months
infections

Sources: Mathematica Policy Research, Inc., and Columbia University, June 18, 1996. Updated
September 22, 1997. Available online:
http://www2.acf.dhhs.gov/programs/hsb/research/index
http://www.acf.dhhs.gov/programs/core/ongoing_research/hs
http://www.mathematicia-mpr.com/3rdlevel/ehstoc

Table 4. Staff Interviews Used in Early Head Start National
Evaluation to Identify Dimensions of Child-Care Quality

Peformace Objective to be Explicated	Indicators to be Explicated	Information Sources
Dimension of Quality	Stability of the child-care setting (child-care centers): e.g., number of adults child interacts with in a typical week; amount of time main provider has cared for child	Caregiver interview @ 14 months; 24 months 36 months
Structural Properties of Quality	Caregiver's education, training, earning from child-care; commitment to the child-care profession	Caregiver interview @ 14 months; 24 months; 36 months
Caregiver's relationship with parents	Perceived relationship with parents	Caregiver interview @ 14 months; 36 months
Caregiver's behavior linked to quality	Caregiver's sensitivity, harshness, and detachment	Caregiver interview @ 14 months; 36 months
Caregiving values and beliefs	Traditional authoritarian beliefs and progressive democratic beliefs	Caregiver interview @ 24 months; 36 months

Sources: Mathematica Policy Research, Inc., and Columbia University, June 18, 1996. Updated September 22, 1997. Available online http://www2.acf.dhhs.gov/programs/hsb/research/index; http://www.acf.dhhs.gov/programs/core/ongoing_research/hs; http://www.mathematicia-mpr.com/3rdlevel/ehstoc

PERSPECTIVE ON FAMILY POLICY

As the twentieth century ended, a number of social policy researchers used the occasion to reflect on lessons learned in studies of family communication and family-institution interaction since 1970, when Lasswell and Dror first proposed the concept of policy sciences and policy analysis (e.g., Lawes 1999; Wallat & Piazza 1997; Zimmerman 1999).

Lasswell (1970) and Dror (1970) conceptualized the role of policy analysts as technicians capable of providing information for legislators and administrators based upon data that had been collected. As Zimmerman and others (e.g., Moroney & Krysik 1998) have pointed out, since 1970 the methodologies available to generate data to address policy questions have expanded beyond surveys and experimental studies. Similar to the study of employment, income, housing, and health, family policy analysts can choose data from any of the following methods, depending on the questions asked by policymakers and administrators: content analyses, computer simulations, historical analyses, cost-benefit studies, regression analyses, and secondary data analysis.

In spite of the availability of multiple theoretical and methodological resources for analyzing program evaluation, program impact, or cost-benefit evaluation against a set of policy standards such as those performance indicators adopted for family-institution interaction programs such as Head Start, a major lesson learned in twentieth century policy research is that there is no guarantee that such information will be used by policymakers and administrators (Wallat & Piazza 1991, 1997).

In her review of family policy research, Zimmerman (1999) wrote that she would stop just short of declaring that she "could not think of one social science finding that was undeniably indispensable in any [family policy] task or effort" (p. 126). Instead she wrote that she would conclude on an optimistic note: Research projects undertaken by "family scholars have been important in documenting social trends and their impacts on family needs and resources" (p. 127). The next step is to accept "the simple fact that there are different ways of perceiving, defining, and investigating policy problems related to families" (p. 116), and to take on the realistic and modest goal of finding ways to concentrate attention on the chief product of family-interaction research that is used by policymakers. That chief product is accounts of communication of policy successes between participants in a program.

In research terms, the chief product is linguistic accounts of situations in which participants were able to override the basic asymmetry of knowledge and communication styles found across all communities and concentrate on interpretations of observations (Zimmerman 1999, pp. 120, 127). (See Tannen & Wallat 1993 for an example of a linguistic account of family-institution interaction.)

As Powell (1994) has noted: "Movements towards conclusive statements about the merits of particular Head Start...practices with specific populations requires research on program variables in context. Here the field consistently comes up short" (p. 242). Perhaps what is needed is a different way of doing family-institution interaction policy research. We now have a decade of theoretical and empirical work on family functioning. We now have convergence across family research fields on a set of referents on family functioning.

As family policy reviewers (e.g., Zimmerman 1999) and family communication researchers (e.g., Lawes 1999) point out, what is needed, and possibly quite useful, is a method that does not assume that all conversational turns in responding to interviews or questionnaires about family functions will display the same meanings for referents identified empirically. Again, this is the kind of information that legislators consider useful. Legislators and administrators ask: What are the effects of publicly funded programs on the ability of family members to perform functions associated with upbringing, such as continuous nurturing of children's social development and time for involvement in children's cognitive development? Qualitative researchers have met the normative purpose of displaying the condition or situation of controlling social behavior, thereby providing models for programs to teach families and staff members how they can start nurturing social development.

The cumulative contribution of the ten-year review presented is fore-grounding the structural characteristics of adult-child talk in social behavior situations (cf. Lawes 1999). Quantitative researchers have met the normative purpose of documenting family functioning tasks accomplished during time available for family interaction (or family talk and communication). The cumulative contribution of qualitative researchers cited in this research monograph is to foreground the semantic content of family functioning tasks (cf. Lawes 1999).

The value of combining the structural and semantic characteristics of both methods is still to be tested in practice. Program evaluation standards, including requirements for interviews with family members and staff, provide a means for validating what have become common terms in the literature (cf. Moroney & Krysik 1998). Designing a comparative analysis of family-institution interaction across program interviews could begin by asking parents and practitioners to include their reactions to available information on observed behaviors and tasks studies to date (such as Table 7), and family functioning terms available from multiple disciplines and fields studying family interaction (such as Table 10). Gathering reactions to research work could well take the form of improved understanding of the long-standing observation that when family-institution interaction exists it is as a discursive form that is in constant flux. "In general, it must be said that although there may be consensus among research findings—and that is encouraging—generalizations from those findings are really only about the *literature,* not about the *real world*" (Clark-Stewart 1977, p. 71). Bringing together parents' and practitioners' comparisons of research generalizations and their own *real world* behaviors and tasks that are constantly in a state of flux can lead to new policy ideas. One policy question would be: What are the effects of family-institution interaction situations on the ability of parents and practitioners to perform functions traditionally associated with parenthood across families?

Given the fact that phrases including developmental change and strengthening and supporting families have had such frequent reinterpretations in policy across the twentieth century (Wallat & Goldman 1979), the proposed use of the decade of research presented in this monograph is more modest perhaps than that to which most family researchers aspire, "but in the face of existing evidence, more realistic as well" (Zimmerman 1999, p. 127).

Contributions developed primarily out of the early childhood intervention and family support efforts of the Administration on Children and Families (ACF) in the late 1960s and early 1970s are the starting point. In a 1978 report on funding of early childhood demonstration projects and sponsored research on the lasting effects of preschool and family support systems by the then-called Administration on Children, Youth and Families (ACYF), reviewers credited ACYF's research as an important precursor in shaping new conceptualizations of the effects of family-institution transactions on child development (Newbrough, Dokecki, Dunlop, Hogge & Simpkins 1978, p. 12). The reviewers noted that such scholarship development "breaks new ground" across the social science disciplines of psychology, anthropology, and sociology: (a) in the consideration of dyadic and group properties associated with biophysical and psychosocial development outcomes; (b) in the consideration of continuity and social change in participation and use of networks or configurations of relatives, friends, extended families, self-help groups, and bureaucracies in order to carry out basic tasks that are the key feature of human development institutions; and (c) in the consideration of how individuals relate to others in dominant institutions of our society.[1]

Based upon their analysis of ACYF directions in the 1970s, Newbrough and his colleagues identified three directions that could build upon ground-breaking work on families as society's primary human development systems, and the impact of societal institutions on the ability to perform that role:

1. Concentrate on both family and child development, and go beyond exclusive concern with the cognitive domain of the child to consider affective and social development (cf. p. 77);

2. Identify or propose methodological aspects for representing interpersonal interactions across development domains (cf. p. 78);

3. Propose a set of family-institution interaction concepts based on features of the structure and organization of activities contributing directly to human development (cf. p. 78)

CHAPTER TWO

Literature Review

A survey and analysis of family research from the following sources will be presented to outline the path for building the new research models and methodologies called for by the ACYF reviewers of work accomplished in the late 1960s and early 1970s. What have researchers already identified as the building blocks of these new research efforts? The review includes: (a) the purposes of studying family situations identified in *Child Development Abstracts* references to family interaction in the ten-year time span 1987–1997, (b) the perspectives on family interaction published in *Family Relations* for the same time period, and (c) explanations of alternative epistemologies and methodologies for the study of relations between people and their environments that have appeared in special issues of *Child Development, Human Development,* and the *Merrill-Palmer Quarterly* in the last decade.

The results of a decade of effort and attention to moving beyond exclusive concern with the cognitive domain to developing ways to think about family functioning across tasks are evident in research projects funded by the Administration on Children and Families (ACF) since 1997. For example, typing in the search term "interaction" in the ACF data base called "Current Head Start and Related Research" (http://www2.acf.dhhs.gov/programs/hsb) provides information on locating projects, contacting principle investigators through the Web, as well as purposes and assessment devices being used. One set of descriptions of twenty projects extending into the year 2002 identifies over 500 measures being used to assess what is assumed to be a combined contribution of family and staff to children's growth and development.

Table 5. Measures Used to Assess Contribution of Family and Staff Members to Children's Growth and Development

Total Measures	Count of Child Focus and Adult Child Focus Measures	Research Contact	Measurement Focused on Child	Adult-Child Interaction as Defined in the Variables Included in the Following Choices of Methods
13	10	New England Research Center on Head Start Quality, Education Development Center, Inc. Newton, MA ddickins@edc.org David Dickinson	●Peabody Picture Vocabulary Test ●Early Phonemic Awareness Profile ●Emergent Literacy Profile ●Book Concepts ●Social and Task Skills Profile ●Social Skills Rating Survey ●Evaluation of Language and Literacy Development ●Child Observation Record (High Scope)	●Teacher-Child Verbal Interaction Profile ●Teacher Language and Culture Questionnaire
36	8	North Carolina Center for Research on Head Start Quality U of North Carolina Chapel Hill bryant@unc.edu Donna Bryant	●Peabody Picture Vocabulary Test ●Woodcock-Johnson Letter-Word Identification ●Woodcock-Johnson Applied Problems ●Early Phonemic Awareness Profile ●Emergent Literacy Profile ●Attitudes/Perceptions of Competence	●Caregiver Interaction Scale ●Interaction Subscale of Assessment Profile for Early Childhood Programs
17	8	Early Head Start (EHS) Research/ Local Research Partner: U of Colorado Health Sciences Center/ Family Star bob.emde@uchsc.edu Robert Emde	●Standard Emotion Events/LAB TAB Tasks ●Empathy ●Preschool Language Scales ●Communicative Development Inventory	●Conflict-Ridden Relationships ●Emotional Availability ●Ethnographic Observation ●Interview of Routines and Caregiving Environment

Total Measures	Count of Child Focus and Adult Child Focus Measures	Research Contact	Measurement Focused on Child	Adult-Child Interaction as Defined in the Variables Included in the Following Choices of Methods
35	5	EHS Local Research Project: Juniper Gardens Children's Project and Project EAGLE carta@kuhub.cc. ukans.edu Judith Carda	●Cognitive and Language Bayley Scales ●Communicative Development Inventories	●Code for Interactive Recording of Caregiving and Learning Environment ●Home Observation for Measurement of the Environment ●Video Protocol
43	10	Pittsburgh EHS / Local Research Project greenb@ch1.ch. pdx.edu Beth Green	●Attachment Q-sort ●Infant Mental Health Assessment ●Self-Efficacy Scale ●Psychological Empowerment Scale	●Parent Behavior Observation Scale ●Observation of Family Experience ●Questions Regarding Parent-Child Relationships ●Parenting Competence Scale ●Ethnographic Case Studies ●Parent-Child Interaction Videotapes
20	6	Project HOME: Home Observation to Measure Effectiveness Iowa State U Dept of Human Development and Family Studies carlapet@iastate.edu Carla A. Peterson	●Bayley Scales of Infant Development, Revised ●Communicative Developmental Inventories ●Child Behavior Checklist	●Home Visit Observation ●Home Visit Critical Incidents ●Supportive Interaction Scale
30	7	EHS and Beyond for Hispanic, Native American, and Other Rural Poor Families in Communities in Washington State U of Washington and Washington State Migrant Council stowi@u.washington.edu Joseph Stowitschek	●Bayley Scales of Infant Development and Behavior ●Adaptive Social Behavior Inventory ●Preschool Language Scale	●Parent-Child Interaction Videotape ●Family Functioning Style ●Provider-Child Observation ●Sample Interval/ Anecdotal Observation

Total Measures	Count of Child Focus and Adult Child Focus Measures	Research Contact	Measurement Focused on Child	Adult-Child Interaction as Defined in the Variables Included in the Following Choices of Methods
30	4	Arkansas EHS Research Project U of Arkansas Affiliated Program Dept of Pediatrics meswanson@goach. uams.edu Mark Swanson	●Grandmother Involvement with Child Scale ●Household Food Environment ●Infant Feeding Questionnaire	●Scales of Intergenerational Relationships Quality
31	9	Attachment in EHS Process and Outcomes U of Washington, School of Nursing kathyb@u.Washington. edu Kathryn Barnard	●Stressful Life Events ●Mastery Scale ●Woodcock-Johnson, Reading ●Strange Situation ●Preschool Language Scales ●Bayley's Mental Development (MDI) Index	●Student-Teacher Relationship Scale ●Nursing Child Assessment Scale ●Home Observation Measurement of the Environment ●Mother Perception of Parent-Child Communication Coaching Activities
11	5	Clayton Mile High Family Futures Project U of Colorado Health Sciences Center Dept of Psychiatry bob.emde@uchsc.edu Robert Emde	●Preschool Language Scales	●Emotional Availability Scale (coded from Videotaped Free Play) ●Observation of Empathy ●Conflict-ridden Relationships ●Home Visitor Ratings of Maternal Involvement
43	10	Local Research Partnership for New York City's EHS Program New York University School of Social Work mes4@is2.nyu.edu Mark Spellman	●Language Development Scale ●Social Skills Rating System ●Developmental Behaviors Checklist for 0–3 ●Dimensions of Temperament Scale ●Peer Play	●Empathy ●Impact of Events ●Maternal Efficacy ●Quality of Stimulation in Home Environment ●Mother-Infant Interaction

Total Measures	Count of Child Focus and Adult Child Focus Measures	Research Contact	Measurement Focused on Child	Adult-Child Interaction as Defined in the Variables Included in the Following Choices of Methods
20	5	Pathways Project: Michigan State U. and the EHS Family Development Program of the Region II Community Action Agency rschiff@ibm.cl.msu.edu Rachael Schiffman	●Emotionality, Adaptability, and Sociability Inventory ●Child and Sibling Health Development	●Nursing Child Assessment ●Dyadic Adjustment Scale ●Home Observation for Measurement of the Environment ●Family Environment Scales
23	8	Harvard Graduate School of Education Early Education Services Research Partnership snowcat@hugsel. harvard.edu Catherine Snow	(Focus is on parent-child interaction as a means to provide information on the impact of the Early Head Start program in order to outline the specific program components shown to produce effects. Parent-child interaction is studied as a context for: 1) language and literacy development 2) socio-emotional development	●Nice and Mean Interaction Scales ●Behavioral Style Communicative Development Inventories ●Book Reading Observation ●Toy Play Observation ●Mastery Task Observation ●Videotape of Parent-Child Toy Tasks ●Videotape and Audiotape of Family Activities
23	5	The Determinants of Later Academic Success of Children Attending Head Start SUNY, Stony Brook gwhitehurst@ccmail. sunysb.edu Grover Whitehurst	●Expressive One-Word Picture Vocabulary Test ●Peabody Picture Vocabulary Test ●Adaptive Language Survey ●Developing Skills Checklist	●Observational Coding for Reading Instruction in Head Start Settings

Total Measures	Count of Child Focus and Adult Child Focus Measures	Research Contact	Measurement Focused on Child	Adult-Child Interaction as Defined in the Variables Included in the Following Choices of Methods
29	7	How Schools and Families Promote the Successful Transition of Children from Head Start to the Public School Classroom Head Start/University Partnership Oklahoma State U Dept of Child Relations and Child Development hubbs@vml.uss. okstate.edu Laura Hubbs-Tait	●Friendship Network ●Social Competence with Peers ●Preschool Social Competence ●Videotaped Peer Interaction Task ●Cognitive Outcomes: Peabody Picture Vocabulary Test; McCarthy Scales of Abilities	●Videotaped Mother-Child Teaching Task Conflict Tactics Scale
25	4	Father's Involvement in the Lives of Head Start Children and Participation in Head Start U of Arkansas Little Rock rhbradley@uslr.edu Robert Bradley	●Medical and Health History ●Language Scale ●Basic Skills Inventory	●Observation of Father-Child Interaction
6	2	Maternal Communication Factors Related to Child Competence U of Georgia lwinn@ugs.cc.uga.edu Laura Winn	●Enact Story Completions	●Videotaped Interaction of Mother Reading to Child
12	5	Early Language Development in Bilingual Environments cruzado@eagle.cc. ukansas.edu Judith Guerrero	●Communicative Development Inventories ●Preschool Language Scale ●Bayley Scales of Infant Development	●Home Observation for Measurement of the Environment ●Code for Interactive Recording of Caregiving and Learning Environment

Total Measures	Count of Child Focus and Adult Child Focus Measures	Research Contact	Measurement Focused on Child	Adult-Child Interaction as Defined in the Variables Included in the Following Choices of Methods
12	4	Enhancement of Child Care Quality and Children's Cognitive and Behavioral Competencies by Providers of Rural Family Child Care Utah State University aaustin@cc.usu.edu Ann Berghout Austin	●Early Language Development ●Basic Concept Scale ●Classroom Behavior	●Caregiver Interaction ●Family Day Care Rating

aThe total number of measures listed in the website description of each Research Project identified in this Table is 443. The average number of measures used across the nineteen Research Project descriptions is twenty-three measures (443 divided by 19=23). Some of the Research Project descriptions include the term interaction under topics such as observations of parents in classrooms. The count of child focus and adult-child focus measures included in Table 5 represents the total titles provided in the project abstracts for measurement focused on the child and adult-child interaction. Other measures listed for each Research Project may provide further information on the project's perspective on "interaction." Hence the description of measures presented in the introduction to the literature review is "over 500 measures." For example, the following twenty-eight titles are not included in Table 5 but are included under measures used in the North Carolina Center for Research on Head Start: Teacher Ratings of Children (Social Skills Rating System, including Problem Behaviors; Adaptive Language Inventory; Student-Teacher Relationship Scale), Parent Interview (Family and Child Experiences Survey[FACES] Interview), Staff Questionnaire (Attitudes About Job; Training Activities; Beliefs About Teaching; Early Childhood; Work Environment Survey; Beliefs About Family Services; Parent Involvement; Health Practices, Demographics), Parent Involvement (Observations of Parent Education Meetings; Observations of Parents in Classrooms; Collection of Monthly Volunteer Data), Health and Safety (Playground Assessment Using Rating Scales Based on Consumer Product Safety; Commission Guidelines; Indoor Classroom Safety Assessment), Goldsboro Follow-up Study (Kindergarten Teacher Checklist, Maryland State Department of Public Instruction; Social Skills Rating System; Student Teacher Relationship Scale; Vineland Adaptive Behavior Scales; Demographic Characteristics of the Teacher), Classroom Observations (Early Childhood Environment Rating Scale; Anti-Bias Environment Checklist; Observation of Hygiene Practices; Observation of Eating Activities; Structural Characteristics of Classroom).

Sources: The information presented in Table 5 is based on a review of content that was identified in November 1999 using the following search steps: (a) go to http://www2.acf.dhhs.gov; (b) arrive at Head Start home page; (c) click on the box called Research that appears on the left side of the page; (d) on the page called Research click on Information on Current Head Start Research and Evaluation Projects; (e) go to http://www.acf. dhhs.gov/cgi-bib/hsre/search to identify hundreds of measures being used in current projects; (f) use the search box available in the section called Select Field. When the word measures appears, type the word Interaction as the keyword in the next search box (e.g., Measures contains Interaction).

SCOPE OF THE REVIEW

Overall, the literature review that follows compiles a view of parallel streams of work in family interaction and organization communication. Bringing these parallel streams together provides a set of comparative indicators for personnel and parents as they consider data collected to meet Performance Standards obligations and other indices of quality that are "regulatable" (Huston 1994).

Building on guidelines for designing and conducting a contrastive review (Cooper 1982; Eisenhart 1998; Jackson 1980; Schwandt 1998), a search of primary data sources to locate family interaction references published in the ten-year period 1987–1997 was conducted. Following McGraw's (1991) advice, a large sample of journals included in *Child Development Abstracts* was used to demonstrate the empirical interests of developmental psychology as well as the continuing calls for illustrating strategies for helping early childhood program participants "see common goals" across child and family studies (Graue 1993, p. 73). As such, the child and family development review sections that follow include: (a) reports on family interaction variables that have been identified in child and family development sources, (b) reports that delve into the implications of family relations for practitioners, and (c) reports that suggest orientations and methodologies for exploring relevant family-institution interaction variables.

The first level of the search for representations of family interaction was reading all Society for Research in Child Development (SRCD) *Abstracts* included in the psychology and theory/methodology sections for the years 1987–1997 (i.e., Volumes 61–71). As Reese (1993) has noted: Previous research of SRCD has "shorted" theory and methodology. The second level of the search was for family interaction articles in all volumes of *Family Relations* published by the National Council on Family Relations for the same time period. The third level of the search was locating special issues on family and child development in three premier journals.

In 1990 *Human Development* published a special issue to help extend psychological accounts of cognitive development to encompass advances in sociological perspectives on human development. In 1992 the *Merrill-Palmer Quarterly* editors organized a special issue on family talk and parent-child relations in an effort to integrate deductive approaches (i.e., experimental designs to capture family interaction) and inductive approaches (i.e., research designs used to address ecological validity definitions and calls for coming to grips with what goes on in day-to-day interactions among family members as well as surrounding caretakers).

A 1994 *Child Development* special issue on family contexts also cast a wide net to address family and society ecological components including economic, educational, political, and ideological dimensions of family institution interaction.[1]

DATA BASES USED TO IDENTIFY STUDIES OF PARENT-CHILD INTERACTION

The 1987–1997 review database for parent-child interaction totaled thirty-five empirical studies located through the "psychiatry, clinical psychology" section of SRCD *Abstracts* Volume 61–Volume 71. These thirty-five studies of family interaction are published in the following twenty-three journals: *Abnormal Child Psychology; Adolescence; American Academy of Child and Adolescent Psychiatry; American Journal on Mental Retardation; Applied Developmental Psychology; Autism and Developmental Disorders; Child Abuse and Neglect; Child and Family Behavior Therapy; Child Care, Health and Development; Child Care Quarterly; Child Development; Child Psychology and Psychiatry; Child Psychology and Psychiatry and Allied Disciplines; Child Welfare; Counseling and Clinical Psychology; Development and Psychopathology; Infant Behavior and Development; Infant Mental Health Journal; Mental Deficiency Research; Orthopsychiatry; Perceptual and Motor Skills; Psychiatry; and Psychological Bulletin.*

The 1987–1997 review database for "theory, methodology" in parent-child interactions comprises twenty-seven primary sources. In contrast to the SRCD "psychiatry, clinical psychology" primary sources on family interaction, the SRCD "theory, methodology" publications on family interaction appeared in the following eighteen journals: *Autism and Developmental Disorders; Child and Family Behavior Therapy; Child Development; Child Psychology and Psychiatry; Child Psychology and Psychiatry and Allied Disciplines; Developmental Review; Human Development; Infant Behavior and Development; Infant Mental Health Journal; Journal of Early Intervention; Journal of Family Issues; Journal of Marriage and the Family; Merrill-Palmer Quarterly; Psychology of Women Quarterly; Psychological Reports; Psychological Review; Social Behavior and Personality; and Topics in Early Childhood Special Education.*

The National Council on Family Relations (NCFR) journal of applied family and child studies includes twenty-six articles on the topic of family interaction for the time period 1987–1997. These parent-child interaction articles were in volumes 36–46 of *Family Relations* (i.e., the volumes published 1987 through 1997). Although *Family Relations* includes articles that report observations of parent-adolescent interaction, these possibilities were omitted because they did not provide a comparative point for observations of family interaction in the early childhood years compiled by using *Child Development Abstracts*.

INITIAL POINTS OF COMPARISON

The most salient comparison feature in the format and purpose of the SRCD and the NCFR data sources is that potential contributors of SRCD articles are told that research reports on family interaction must address "research implications" and the *Family Relations* editorial board requires that all articles must provide implications for clinical practice and interventions with family members. These purposes are apparent in reading through the articles (See Tables 6 and 7).

As demonstrated in Table 6 and Table 7, the dominant purpose identified in the thirty-five SRCD "psychiatry, clinical psychology" observational studies is cast in terms of how each study builds on, or replicates, or extends past work on the interaction function represented as verbal communicative control of social behavior and language development. Table 6 includes all of the family interaction observational studies included in the more detailed compilation of the content of these studies in the next section.

The observational studies identified by study purpose in Table 6 can also be presented as a composite of major design components that were found across all of the family interaction studies referenced in *Abstracts* under "psychiatry, clinical psychology." One reason for presenting a compilation of the variables used to identify and explicate "interaction," and the tasks accomplished during this interaction, is to illustrate an observation paradigm that remained dominant for the ten-year period 1987–1997 in the study of family interaction. As mentioned earlier, the SRCD "psychiatry, clinical psychology" set of primary sources were located in twenty-three early childhood journals. This range of sources provides documentation that there is an extensive number of publications limited to an analysis of family interaction as a set of control and direct teaching strategies. Since research methodologies appear to be influenced by the goals of researchers, the purposes of each author or group of authors are summarized in Table 7.

Table 7 illustrates design features of family interaction research across one set of child and development sources across a ten-year span. The total sample of parents in thirty-five studies recorded in the "psychiatry, clinical psychology" category for the ten-year period 1987–1997 ranged from 1 to over 300.[2] The age of the children ranged from three days old to eight years with a total sample of 807 early childhood children one month to three years old, 702 children three to five years old, and 489 children six to eight years old. Three studies reported participation by mothers and fathers while 85 percent of the studies addressed mothers' interaction with their children.

The family interaction behavior variables included in Table 7 were based upon observation periods that ranged from three minutes to a four-hour home observation. Although differences in age and task(s) performed are apparent in the columns labeled as such, the majority of these studies defined "interaction" as parents' manifestations of control. The parents were rated on use of verbal praise, use of commands or directives, and use of contingent responses or nonpunitive control. The representations of family interaction included by contributors identified in the "psychiatry, clinical psychology" index category are quite narrow.

In other words, out of a range of multiple functions of interaction researchers have identified as universal human resources (cf., Wallat 1984), and variable upbringing functions identified by *Family Relations* contributors (e.g., Johnston 1990; Lauer & Lauer 1991; Visher & Visher 1989), the twenty-three SRCD journals which report parent-child interaction studies are devoting significant space to research on one function of family interaction.

Overall, the observation study components outlined in Table 7 continue the tradition of simplifying the complex task of studying "interaction." The thirty-five studies identified in Table 7 used an average of five subcategories to create a representation of parent-child interaction. The authors' discussion of the observed behavior variables presented in Table 7 do not address whether or not researchers think these units of analysis correlate with every family's expectations about their own or their child's interaction format (i.e., their beliefs about customary usage or manner or way of acting, doing, or being). Little mention is made of additional functions of interaction young children are capable of displaying through language, or the variation in meaning that the children and adults who served as subjects would give to the nonverbal and verbal communication examples researchers represent as control, compliance, and so forth (cf. Wallat 1984, 1991a; Wallat & Piazza 1988).

Table 6. Purposes of Family Interaction Research
Across SRCD Primary Sources in "Psychiatry,
Clinical Psychology"

SOURCE	SCOPE OF RESEARCH	PURPOSE OF RESEARCH
Alvey & Aeschleman 1990	teach parents teaching interactions	Implement parent training program to teach mothers to learn a script and use verbal praise reinforcers in their interactions with their child.
Baird et al. 1992	facilitate new understandings of the link between assessment and intervention	Develop an assessment of infant-parent interaction that can display co-occurring interactive patterns in contrast to frequency of each individual's interaction.
Barkley 1988	investigate methylphenidate effects by observing mother–preschool child interactions	Extend previous research by more closely assessing whether mothers will "soften" their management style (i.e., "soften" management style defined as reducing use of directives and commands as child's compliance rate increases when they are on medication).
Barkley 1989	investigate ritalin effects by observing mother–six-year-old child interactions	Replicate study of "softening" management style with a six-year-old sample taking Ritalin.
Becker & Becker 1994	develop a maternal behavior inventory to capture multiple indicators of mother-to-infant attachment	Illustrate how studies can determine the psychometric properties of a number of maternal behaviors to assess to what extent those psychometric properties vary across infant gender.
Beckwith 1988	preterm infants' and mothers' level of responsive interactions	Develop intervention program to increase the rate of mothers' observation of her infant and her use of contingent responses.
Campbell et al. 1987	mother-child conflict interactions during play	Illustrate quantitative and qualitative categories that may be used to help connect observation of discrete control and noncompliance behavior categories with "global qualitative features" of mother-child conflict and cooperation (e.g., "global qualitative feature" defined as use of persuasive affective tone).
Cerezo et al. 1996	interactional patterns of child physical abuse	To consider the differentiating aspects of the abusive mother's and the nonabusive mother's behavior toward their children.

Continued on next page

SOURCE	SCOPE OF RESEARCH	PURPOSE OF RESEARCH
Chatoor et al. 1988	mother-infant feeding and play interactions	Consider variation in conflict and struggle for control by observing attempts by mothers to deal with infant anorexia nervosa (i.e., conflict and struggle for control defined as child's temperament and mother's inconsistency in forcing or not forcing bottle or food into infant's mouth).
Cramer & Stern 1988	case study evaluation of changes in mother-infant interaction during "brief" therapy	Identify how interactional variables (i.e., mother's agression, physical closeness, face-to-face orientation toward infant) may be tied, or may correspond, to maternal interpretations of child's behavior.
DiLalla & Crittenden 1990	social interaction among abusing and neglecting parents and their children	Provide a common language in order to represent "global organization of behavior" categories from at-home observations in contrast to the wide array of molecular behavior categories used to date across studies.
Drotar et al. 1990	maternal interactional behavior with nonorganic failure-to-thrive six-month old infants	Identify variables related to measurement of maternal interaction behaviors (i.e., use a combination of discrete interactional behaviors during feeding, discrete home environment features, plus qualitative dimensions of maternal sensitivity to infant).
Dumas et al. 1989a	clusters of mother-child interaction behavior associated with maternal distress and child maladjustment	Address the contradictory findings of studies which point to: expression of depressive symptoms by mothers as associated with increased compliance and/or increased conduct disorders (i.e., consider deviance as a behavior exhibited in different manner across situation).
Dumas & Lechowicz 1989b	mother-child and father-child interactional measures in conduct-disorder children	Address past studies that suggest that child compliance can be significantly increased by teaching caregivers to issue clear-cut commands (i.e., demonstrate that the relative importance and type and quality of commands by mothers and fathers remains unclear and poorly understood: suggestions or direct instructions may not always lead to more direct compliance).

Continued on next page

SOURCE	SCOPE OF RESEARCH	PURPOSE OF RESEARCH
Eyberg 1988	parent-child interaction therapy	Illustrate a behavioral therapy approach that integrates child play therapy techniques with behavior management skills (i.e., list of do's and don'ts, including, do not ask questions that are clearly implied commands or that direct choices and decisions about the game being played).
Floyd & Phillippe 1993	interactions of mothers and fathers with their school-age children with mild to moderate mental retardation	Test the hypothesis that because children with mental retardation have learning difficulties and limited psychological skills that make special demands on their parents, the parent-child interactions will be marked by (a) more frequent behavior management struggles, (b) more coerciveness, and (c) fewer positive exchanges as compared with a group of families with children who do not have mental retardation.
Gardner 1987	interaction between mothers and conduct-problem children	Address the lack in knowledge of variable types of activities families engage in in addition to the 5 percent of conflict time studied so frequently (i.e., illustrate a next step by describing mothers' skill in structuring a joint activity and keeping it going with use of "sensitive and subtle control means").
Hamilton et al. 1993	mothers' and children's interaction style in conflict solving	Examine the association between child communication coping style (CS), defined as assessing alternative ways an eight-year-old can respond to emotional atmosphere of the family, and maternal affective style (A), indexed by parental criticism and guilt-induction.
Haynes-Seman 1987	developmental origins of psychopathology	Observe toddlers' interactions with mothers, and conduct interviews to address the following: What abuse or neglect patterns of parenting may be transmitted from early experiences? What mother-child interactions and experiences during mealtime, diapering, and playtime can be identified in terms of parents' attention and reciprocity? How does the parent interpret/explain the child's behavior during these activities?

Continued on next page

SOURCE	SCOPE OF RESEARCH	PURPOSE OF RESEARCH
Hecht et al. 1993	characteristics of conversations between mothers and their preschool children with developmental delays	Compare the conversational characteristics associated with different situations (naturally occurring versus semi-structured) and different activities (task-like versus play) to better understand the nature of goals, interpretations, and participant structures that are visible in situations that are qualitatively different.
Heermann et al. 1994	maternal and paternal parent-child interaction	Report the factor analyses of the Ainsworth scales used to rate both maternal and paternal behavior during interaction with their infants at one, six, and twelve months of age.
Hoffman & Drotar 1991	optimal mother–infant interaction	Reexamine the question: Like mother like baby? and test hypotheses related to the finding that infants of mildly to moderately depressed mothers, like their mothers, show less positive affect and a narrower range of emotion than infants of nondepressed mothers.
Howlin & Rutter 1989	autistic children's socialized language patterns and parents' eliciting utterances communication style	Teach parents of autistic children to make greater use of linguistic structures that are associated with language development.
Johnston & Pelham 1990	mother-child interactions in families of children with externalizing disorders	Design research to solve the difficulty of observings links between parenting behavior, children's disorders, and maternal characteristics (e.g., self-esteem, depressive symptoms, marital satisfaction) by demonstrating correlations between researcher's ratings of child behavior and mothers' ratings of how typical the interaction has been.
Kasari et al. 1988	caregivers' attention and behavior regulation interactions with children	Compare mothers' and fathers' interactions with four-year-old autistic and mentally retarded children to caregivers' interactions with two-year-olds with mental age similar to the four-year-old autistic and mentally retarded children (Catelle or Stanford-Binet scores).
Kasari et al. 1995	attention regulation of children with Down Syndrome and children with typical development	Explore instances of attention regulation exhibited by children (i.e., attention regulation as: (a) coordinated joint attention towards object and adult, and (b) social referencing looks towards object and adult.

Continued on next page

SOURCE	SCOPE OF RESEARCH	PURPOSE OF RESEARCH
Koester 1995	face-to-face interaction between hearing mothers and their deaf or hearing infants	Examine patterns of face-to-face interaction between deaf and hearing nine-month-old infants and their mothers, to determine which infant behaviors are most affected by lack of access to the auditory channel of communication.
Konstantareas et al. 1988	maternal speech to children	Move beyond counting the total number of mother-child utterances to identify the pattern of linguistic input, and hence, communication patterns sensitive to children's competence levels (i.e., patterns of answering questions, asking questions using language modeling, using directives, using shorter lengths of utterances).
Olson et al. 1990	precursors of children's impulse control	Observe parent-toddler "responsive, cognitively stimulating interactions" to address the question, "Do seven composite 'quality' indicators of mother-toddler interaction predict individual differences in children's impulsivity over a four-year period?"
Pianta et al. 1987	mother-child interactions in teaching situations	Illustrate how mothers' (a) structuring of teaching situations, (b) management of problem solving during teaching, and (c) "quality" of instruction assistance can be used to trace changes in family patterns which account for developmental outcomes.
Polansky et al. 1992	scale maternal characteristics of relatedness, impulse control, verbal accessibility, child neglect	Conduct a cross-validation of the Maternal Characteristics Scale with new and more diverse samples of both mothers and practitioners. The Maternal Characteristics Scale is a device for codifying and rendering quantifiable information acquired by practitioners in the ordinary course of their work.
Shapiro et al. 1987	family interaction as "communicative, synchronous dialogue, interaction" between mothers and their autistic children	Demonstrate how observing parents' application of methods to set up a dialogue with their autistic child provides an observation tool that can be useful to studying mother-child interaction with other families in other settings.

Continued on next page

SOURCE	SCOPE OF RESEARCH	PURPOSE OF RESEARCH
Strayhorn & Weidman 1989	parent-preschooler interaction training	Illustrate how teaching parents teaching interactions, i.e., methods to improve their skill in rating symptoms of attention deficit, and methods to increase their use of a "Parent Practice Scale," can be maximized by employment of trainers whose cultural background helps training program establish rapport with low-income, high-risk parents.
Webster-Stratton 1988	mothers' and fathers' command interactions with children	Reexamine 1970s findings that report that there are significant differences between mothers' and fathers' use of commands in their interactions with conduct-problem children (i.e., findings of "no significance" in this study may reflect a generational change in the role of the father).

Source: Ten-year review of primary sources identified through use of *Child Development Abstracts* "psychiatry, clinical psychology" section, 1987–1997, Volumes 61–71.

Table 7. Compilation of Interpretative Review Components

Author	Observed Behavior(s)	Observation Time	Task(s) Performed	Age	Size of Sample
Alvey & Aeschleman 1990	maternal use of reinforcers (verbal praise)	2–5 hr. training session	learn verbal praise examples	7, 8 yrs.	2
Baird et al. 1992	infant-parent social interaction codes parent: contingent directiveness intrusiveness facilitation infant: initiation participation (i.e., lack of frowning, crying, or turning away) signal clarity intentional	5 minutes	mothers asked to "play" as you normally do when you are not feeding, bathing, or changing your infant	7 month mean age	159
Barkley 1988	maternal commands: command-question question praise negative reaction no response child behaviors: compliance competing (off-task) negative interaction independent play no response	20 minutes	5 tasks in clinic playroom: pick up toys copy design complete counting problems draw a line through a maze play independently	3–4 yrs.	27
Barkley 1989	interactions: mother commands child complies mother praises	20 minutes	<same as above>	6 yrs.	40
Becker & Becker 1992	indicators of attachment: tactile contact visual contact verbal contact responds to infant's need	5 minutes	feeding	3 days old	200
Beckwith 1988	categories of responsiveness: talking talking in face holding mutual visual regard contingency to distress	n/r	develop observation skills	infants	35

Continued on next page

Author	Observed Behavior(s)	Observation Time	Task(s) Performed	Age	Size of Sample
Campbell et al. 1987	maternal structuring: directives praise suggests alternatives control child behaviors: negative non-compliant aggressive	15 min.	play with child as you would at home (lab had 9 toys)	2–3 yrs.	64
Cerezo et al. 1996	interaction variables mother: neutral approach neutral instructions positive instructions aversive response child: prosocial deviant	avg. of 7 times for 1 hour	family told to behave as they usually did	8 yrs. avg.	47
Chatoor et al. 1988	interaction variables mother: positioned for reciprocal exchange talk positive remarks child: distracted cried turned away	20 min.	recreate as closely as possible the at-home feeding experience	20 month	42
Cramer & Stern 1988	types of parent responses: positive responses (all maternal actions & interpretations of child's action as normal assertiveness, curiosity, exploration) avoidant responses aversive responses	5 therapy sessions	mother and infant attend psychotherapy sessions together	10 month	1
Di Lalla & Crittenden, 1990	positive social interaction: caretaking discipline refusal hostility	1 min.	"free activity" in the family's home	2.3 yrs.	20
Drotar et al. 1990	discrete interactive behavior during feeding (timing, pacing, termination)	n. s.	feeding at home	6 month	20

Continued on next page

Author	Observed Behavior(s)	Observation Time	Task(s) Performed	Age	Size of Sample
Dumas et al. 1989a	interactions which form the following clusters of m/c behaviors: m adversive (disappointing & questioning behaviors) c adversive (annoying & aggressive behaviors) m positive (rewarding & approving behaviors) c positive (helping or neutral behaviors accompanied by positive affect)	4 one-hour observations	child's home ("go about daily routine" but no TV or phone calls)	6 yrs. (mean)	33
Dumas & Lechowicz 1989b	different commands (e.g., direct commands, indirect commands, prescribes)	2 one-hour observations	child's home ("go about daily routine," but no TV or phone calls)	6.3 yrs. (mean)	22 mothers and fathers
Eyberg 1988	interaction rules don't rules: indirect commands unlabeled praise do rules: describe what child is doing imitate what child is doing repeat, or rephrase what child is doing	practice 5 minutes per day	play with child while wearing a bug-in-ear device through which author coached parents	pre-school	n.s.
Floyd & Phillippe 1993	interaction clusters: positive—positive verbal endearments, holding negative—physical aggression, verbal attack, coercion neutral—clear request	2 observations of 2 hours	family activity (e.g., dinner, cleaning up, baking cookies, family crafts)	6–18 yrs.	53
Gardner 1987	activity codes joint activity joint conversation play alone sub play talk maintenance TV angry conflict control sib-fight rough-and-tumble	4 times 4 hours total	get on with whatever they normally do (no rules re: phone, TV)	4 yrs. (mean)	39

Continued on next page

Author	Observed Behavior(s)	Observation Time	Task(s) Performed	Age	Size of Sample
Hamilton et al. 1993	mother's affective style profile: supportive guilt inducing criticism criticism of situation personal criticism Child's Coping Style Profile: self affirmation guilt inducing criticism refusal self denigration	5 minutes	Conflict Resolution Task: Mother and child generate a list of topics they disagree upon but are willing to try to reach agreement on. One topic selected by researchers to be the focus of m/c interaction	8–16 yrs.	64
Haynes-Seman 1987	functions accomplished during interaction (no pre-coding categories)	n.s.	meal, diapering, play	2.5 yrs.	1
Hecht et al. 1993	mother and child language use: commands requests comments (i.e., labels, descriptions, statement of rules)	4 hours x 2 days	4 Types of Activities: naturally occurring play, semi-structured play (doll), naturally occurring task activities (e.g., bathing, dressing), semi-structured tasks (i.e., show pairing, clothes sorting)	3.2 yrs.	30
Heermann et al. 1994	infant-parent interaction kinesthetic sensory stimulation	5 minutes at 1 month of age, 10 minutes at 6 months of age, 12 minutes at 12 months	interact with infant doing anything they wished with the exception of feeding	first year	310
Hoffman & Drotar 1991	maternal: affectionate physical contact contingent responding distress-reducing physical contact facilitate involvement with toy contingent responding with toy infant: contingent responding involvement with toy	10 min.	free play in a laboratory playroom	2 month	22

Continued on next page

Author	Observed Behavior(s)	Observation Time	Task(s) Performed	Age	Size of Sample
Howlin & Rutter 1989	maternal use of 10 "language development" directed utterances child use of 7 socialized utterances: echoes questions questions/answers spontaneous directions/commands	weekly home visits for 6 months, then biweekly for 12 months	maternal interactions: questions answers limitations echoes reductions expansions mimicry corrections reinforcements	6.5 yrs. (mean)	16
Johnston & Pelham 1990	maternal direction of interaction: praises nominations child compliance of interaction: negative independent activity	20 min.	5 tasks: delay snack; pick up toys; complete maze; arrange block design; complete math problem	8 yrs. (mean)	40
Kasari et al. 1988	attention regulation behavior regulation responsiveness	12 min.	5 tasks: lab playroom (play with any of 9 toys; play with doll, bed, & bottles; play with puzzles; play without toys; put toys away)	4.5 yrs. 2.5 yrs.	36 18
Kasari et al. 1995	engage in coordinated attention (2) sequences of coordinated attention: looks to adult looks to toys	n.s.	present child with different toys	13–42 month	58
Koester 1995	types of attempts to engage parent: rhythmic (e.g., cycling feet, kicking, waving arms, rocking, closing/opening fists) affect cues (smile, frown) observe (watch mother) signal/reach look away vocalize	3 minutes	tasks performed by adult (a) turn away from infant (b) face infant with "still face" (c) resume as in task one	9 month	40

Continued on next page

Author	Observed Behavior(s)	Observation Time	Task(s) Performed	Age	Size of Sample
Konstrantareas et al. 1988	maternal: directives control reinforcement for motor behavior questions answers reinforcement for child's spoken utterances (i.e., expansions, corrections of child's verbalization)	15 min.	interact as you would at home	6 yrs. (mean)	20
Olson et al. 1990	warm responsiveness avoidance of restriction responsiveness nonrestrictive attachment security verbal stimulation nonpunitive control	2 three-hour home	Child—4 tasks: matching, drawing, walking, delay of present opening observations	6 yrs.	80
Pianta et al. 1987	maternal: supportive presence quality instructional assistance structuring of the situation hostility toward child confidence in dealing with the task child: persistence enthusiasm negative affect compliance reliance dependency affection avoidance	n.s.	teaching in 4 problem-solving situations: copy block pattern; name objects with wheels; place objects according to color and shape; trace a maze	3.5 yrs.	267
Polansky et al. 1992	maternal characteristics scale 4 traits: Relatedness Impulse Control Confidence Verbal Accessibility	n.s.	descriptive statements rated by caseworkers based on behaviors observed	3–5-year-olds	51
Shapiro et al. 1987	set up dialogues with child	3 ten-minute segments	play lab	3.3 yrs. (mean)	5

Continued on next page

Author	Observed Behavior(s)	Observation Time	Task(s) Performed	Age	Size of Sample
Strayhorn & Weidman 1989	communicates enthusiasm gives approval non-directive conversation plays imaginatively	25 min.	teach child elements of curriculum developed by researchers	3.9 yrs. (mean)	41
Webster-Stratton 1988	parent: command criticism child: deviance noncompliance	30 minutes for 2 evenings	maintain home routine as much as possible (but no TV or phone)	5.5 yrs. (mean)	85 mothers and fathers
Yogman 1995	father interaction/ involvement with infants living with child and mother, plays with child	mother's report to interviewer	fathers' play with infants is distinct: tends to be more stimulating, vigorous, arousing, than play between mothers and infants	father involvement in play and caregiving at 12, 24, & 36 months	985 self reports

Key
n/r   not reported
n.s.   not specified

Source: Ten-year review of primary sources identified through use of *Child Development Abstracts* "psychiatry, clinical psychology" section, 1987–1997, Volumes 61–71.

The reasons for continuing to design interaction studies based upon a very limited number of variables are invisible across the SRCD "psychiatry, clinical psychology" research set. This analysis of the ten-year set of adult-child interaction studies suggests that the frame of reference on family communication repeated throughout the journals identified above represents the value system that parenting should look like the asymmetrical social interaction structure of school teaching (i.e., adult initiates, child responds, adult praises or evaluates).

This sequence of one adult controlling the topics initiated as well as the interpretation and valuing of the children's forthcoming response has been consistently identified in studies of classroom interaction. Reviewers of classroom interaction studies describe this organization of interaction as taking up 75 percent of the school day (Edwards & Westgate 1994). In her critique of parent-child interaction studies, Eyberg (1988) concludes that the sorts of interaction represented as parent initiates or directs, child responds, parent provides feedback, evaluates, or praises, may or may not be effective in explicating the nature of family functioning. She points out that conflict periods, or direct teaching periods, take up about 5 percent of how families that include conduct-problem children spend their time. The nature and substance of family interaction during 95 percent of the time is open to question (Eyberg 1988).

More recently, Rogoff and Toma (1997) reviewed twenty years of research on parent-child interaction and reached a conclusion similar to Eyberg's. Their aim is to report observations conducted across cultures that indicate mutual engagement of children and caregivers in everyday problem solving. They are not suggesting that a format of shared thinking should simply replace the prevailing transmit-and-test-receipt-of-information format reported about U. S. families, but that people learn to engage in different formats of social interaction for different purposes.

Although SRCD contributors Gardner (1987), Haynes-Seman (1987), and Howlin & Rutter (1989) attempted to capture a range of activities, the eighty-seven observed behavior categories used in eighteen research studies both implicitly and explicitly communicate that the format that counts in "psychiatry, clinical psychology" research is parents' manifestations of control, and how they manage or deal with lack of compliance (Alvey & Aeschleman 1990; Barkley 1988, 1989; Beckwith 1988; Campbell, Breaux, Ewing, Szumowski, & Pierce 1987; Cerezo, D'Ocon, & Dolz 1996; Chatoor, Egan, Getson, Menvielle, & O'Donnell 1988; Cramer & Stern 1988; DiLalla & Crittenden 1990; Dumas, Gibson, & Albin 1989a; Dumas & Lechowicz 1989b; Floyd & Phillippe 1993; Hecht, Levine, & Mastergeorg 1993; Hoffman & Drotar 1991; Johnston & Pelham 1990; Kasari, Sigman, Mundy, & Yirmiya 1988; Konstrantareas, Zajdeman, Homatidid, & McCabe 1988; Webster-Stratton 1988). The continued attempt to label parent control across a decade of child development work perpetuates a frame of reference that emphasizes locating behaviors within individuals rather than investigating the possibility of locating the details of organization of control and compliance in situations (cf. Erickson 1975a; Cook-Gumperz 1995).

While it is true that eleven of the articles mentioned above included criticisms of behavior categories generally used to observe adult-child interaction, none of the authors explicitly discussed the theoretical implication of the order of their own presentation of parent behavior categories (Ochs 1979). In the absence of such discussion, the authors of all eleven articles implicitly uphold a professional culture notion of the adult as the originator of dominance and control, despite inclusion of statements such as: (a) Conflicts are greatest during task situations rather than free play; and (b) Conflict in mother-child interaction may stem from the severity of the child's condition or disorder systems rather than from poor management skills of the mother (cf. Barkley 1988; Barkley 1989; Beckwith 1988; Campbell, Breaux, Ewing, Szumowski, & Pierce 1987; Chatoor, Egan, Getson, Menvielle, & O'Donnell 1987; DiLalla & Crittenden 1990; Drotar, Eckerle,

Satola, Pallotta, & Wyatt 1990; Dumas, Gibson, & Albin 1989a; Dumas & Lechowicz 1989b; Johnston & Pelham 1990; Kasari, Sigman, Mundy, & Yirmiya 1988).

Looking down the list of Table 7 interaction variables included in column 2, readers will, however, find seven studies that attempted to address properties of the methods and procedures families use to accomplish the task of establishing strategies for interacting with others (cf. Sabatelli & Bartle 1995). For example, Shapiro, Frosch, and Arnold (1987) attempt to address the problem of lack of "measures available to determine progress in interaction and socialization" (p. 485). They refer readers to "good evidence" (p. 485) that dyadic joint attention facilitates language learning. By "good evidence" they refer readers to the results of work that began in the late 1960s that suggests that verbal interchange skill can be traced back in the unfolding of linguistic performance in parent-child interaction history.

These two theoretical statements on the progress of socialization over time and the unfolding of linguistic performance over time clearly index an interest in investigating the development of family interaction as both a content and a social process (cf. Wallat 1991b).

Questions about the unfolding of linguistic performance in family interaction is addressed in later studies of parent-infant interaction completed by Baird, Haas, McCormick, Carruth, & Turner (1992), Becker & Becker (1994), Drotar, Eckerle, Satola, Pallotta, & Wyatt (1990), Heermann, Jones, & Wikoff (1994), Kasari, Freeman, Mundy, & Sigman (1995) and Koester (1995). One of the points made by Baird, Haas, McCormick, Carruth, and Turner (1992) is that representations of child initiation and parent communicative acts are evolving in family interaction observations. They demonstrated the possibility of building on past work to consider performance of intentions by preschool-age children. Such measurement advances lead to new images of communicative acts, i.e., the acts performed in the making of an utterance (cf. Searle 1969). One example of studies that Baird and his colleagues suggested would be useful has been reported in language development literature. During the 1970s researchers attempted to determine if it was possible to categorize a preschool child's intentions from transcripts of talk across day care, home, and community settings. Their measurement yielded a corpus of six general categories—and thirty-two different types—of speech acts: (a) requests for information, action, or acknowledgment, (b) direct responses to preceding utterances, (c) descriptions of observable aspects of the context, (d) statements expressing analytical or institutional beliefs, attitudes, reasons, (e) acknowledgments regulating contact and conversation, and (f) organizational devices that accomplished an act (Miller 1977).

One immediate benefit of new representations of interaction based upon a definition of the *PERFORMANCE* and *SITUATION* being observed is developing new knowledge on diverse courses of development in contrast to the assumption that the causes of development are similar or identical across families (Eisenberg 1992). Citations included in SRCD theory, methodology references for the ten-year period 1987–1997, argue for such expansions of frames of reference in current ideas about family functioning. Such directions are possible to identify from recent efforts aimed at recreating a research focus on units of analysis and variables to explicate the importance of considering *SITUATION*.

The recent publication of available representations of "social fields," including the possibilities of demonstrating the characteristics of *SITUATION* as social and/or structural properties within processes or relations between parts, is an example of such efforts in psychiatry and psychology to "catch up to where Kurt Lewin had been 80 years ago" (Gold 1999, p.15). Capturing the richness of the social organization of families' performing of tasks, and the "lifespace" within which persons alter their behavior, involves examining what social context of family institution interaction has (e.g., the sense of direction of relationships through use of concepts such as systems of meaning and interpretation, historical influence, culture, social support), and what social context of family institution interaction does (e.g., the uses of social interaction such as participating in complex systems and performance of a variety of tasks, styles, and routines across these systems, cf. Wallat 1991b).

The following authors of two of the thirty-five SRCD "psychiatry, clinical psychology" articles during the ten-year period under review did mention the need to support work which illustrates the importance of considering *SITUATION*, in order to address why children do not express deviance in the same manner across all observations. Campbell, Breaux, Ewing, Szumowski, and Pierce (1987) explained their findings of mothers' continued use of negative control "despite improvements in their children's behavior" (p. 438) as underscoring calls to consider parent expectations and situational factors. Dumas, Gibson, and Albin (1989a) stated that "when their mothers are distressed, these [thirty-three] children are more deviant but they do not exhibit their deviance in the same manner across all social situations" (p. 520). In other words, children are selectively maladjusted. "The extent of their deviance depends on the situation in which they are evaluated" (p. 520).

Although these references to variability across situations were published in the late 1980s, theoretical and methodological possibilities to build on such findings were just beginning.

CHILD DEVELOPMENT JOURNALS:
THEORY, METHODOLOGY CONTRIBUTIONS

The SRCD "theory, methodology" articles do not negate the purposes of the "psychiatry, clinical psychology" work. Rather, authors of work which is abstracted in the SRCD "theory, methodology" category attempt to persuade readers to address new questions that stem from research reports on variability across families' institutional settings. Examples of the "theory, methodology" questions raised in the 1987–1997 time period under review included: Why does the emphasis on verbal language focus mainly on children's commitment to cooperation? What will the early childhood function of cooperation change to with age? What may happen if children do not have opportunities to use the repertoire of human language functions? Why have decades of programmatic research on problematic family interaction (e.g., Patterson and his colleagues) not influenced the adoption of methods that have demonstrated the value of analysis of microsocial processes (i.e., a term used to denote close face-to-face interaction) in explicating many different mechanisms through which control or conflict may function?

It should be pointed out that presenting points of contrast between the set of SRCD "psychiatry, clinical psychology" primary sources and the SRCD "theoretical and methodological" sources on family interaction is not intended to suggest that social science research should pick another topic besides power and control. Rather, the contrastive analysis is intended to provide a glimpse of a range of alternative perspectives for considering organizing interaction over time. McGraw (1991) demonstrated in his review of the empirical interests of development psychology across journals that trends can be identified in the interests of a discipline. Reading all of the *Abstracts* in the "theory, methodology" category led to twenty-seven publications that specify new directions in family interaction.[3]

Based on a content analysis of authors' statements about new directions needed in family research, the overall purposes of the SRCD "theory, methodology" publications on family interaction in the early childhood years can be compiled into three themes: (a) enduring measurement and analysis problems, (b) convergence of interest in creating conceptual frameworks such as family as a social system to further our understanding of development, and (c) designing empirical studies of children's and families' participation in different service models with attention to diversity. A specific reference for each of these themes is presented in Table 8.

Overall, the contributors to "theory, methodology" mentioned in Table 8 provide support to developing conceptualizations of both children and adults learning to become participants in a family social system. Adopting such a perspective provides opportunities for researchers and practitioners to be attentive to how children influence the organization and functions of social systems such as the family and peer groups in child-care arrangements (Duncan 1991; Wallat & Piazza 1988). Such guiding perspectives lead to further investigations of family interaction as a *SITUATION* that can be investigated by identifying features of organization and features of family members' interaction across physical space and social space. "Thus the child cannot be abstracted from the family and the family cannot be disconnected from the cultural, political, and economic institutions that establish the boundaries of the family system" (Furstenberg 1985, p. 281).

The research and practice implication of such findings is clear: What is it about parent-professional interaction that constitutes effectiveness? It is finding ways to address such implications that is a major purpose of the National Council for Family Relations contributions presented in the next section.

Table 8. Theory, Methodology Themes

Measurement and Analysis Problems

Explicate variation in function and structure of family interactions (i.e., breadth and complexity of family interaction).	Eyberg 1988
Identify processes as continuous and discontinuous.	Birkel, Lerner, & Smyer 1989
Measure what can go on to facilitate optimizing development in varying contexts.	Brandtstader 1990
Explicate change in children, families, and different service models across contexts (situations).	Hauser-Cram & Krauss 1991
Move beyond frequency counts of individual utterances by adult and child (i.e., identify co-occurring interaction patterns building upon theories of intention and speech acts).	Baird, Haas, McCormick, Carruth, & Turner 1992
Convey what a developmental theory must be able to do to be adequate (i.e., what other kinds of valid explanations besides causal explanations may account for developmental constraints).	Campbell & Bickhard 1992
Develop classifications of pervasive developmental disorders.	Rutter & Schopler 1992
Direct research attention to the ways adults and children experience development (i.e., consider complexity of human behavior and expanding units of relationships; consider indeterminacy and uncertainty and limited predictability in human behavior).	Emde 1994
Measure intragroup and intergroup processes of socialization outside the family (influences of relationships on relationships: the parental relationship, the sibling relationship).	Harris 1995
Identify parents' evaluations of their own role performance across an array of parenting responsibilities.	Sabatelli & Waldron 1995
Recognize that the small set of commonly accepted measures of family characteristics, structure, and process are rather crude proxies for circumstances and processes that may or may not be occurring in the family.	Teachman 1995
Examine parental influences of both fathers and mothers on child development.	Phares 1996

Conceptual Frameworks

the structure of social institutions as shaped by social processes including continuity and change	Chapman 1990
concepts of environment, including macro and micro levels and types of organization systems, interaction systems	Dannerfer & Perlmutter 1990
complex forms and products of social interaction across social systems	Fetterman & Marks 1990
family as social system (i.e., family interaction as features of organization of situation)	Duncan 1991

Continued on next page

developmental psychology as reflection of philosophies of science or worldview	Reese 1993
proximal aspects of caregiving systems (i.e., classify the elements of caregiving according to functions of caregiving acts and the forms acts take)	Bradley & Caldwell 1995

Designing Studies of Diversity

Include diverse samples in family interaction, intervention, and competence studies.	Benasich et al. 1992 Coplin & Hlouts 1991 Doise 1990 Entwistle & Astone 1994 Hauser 1994 Laosa 1989 Sugland et al. 1995
Orient considerations of development to individual's ways of knowing (e.g., sensorimotor affective knowledge emerging from birth to eight months, abstract or symbolic knowledge emerging from approximately eighteen months).	Lewis 1991
Identify cultural images and representations of the socially constructed nature of fatherhood and fatherhood norms and values, the beliefs surrounding the social status of father and its associated roles.	Marsiglio 1993

Source: Ten-year review of primary sources identified through use of *Child Development Abstracts* "theory, methodology" section, 1987–1997, Volumes 61–71.

FAMILY RELATIONS: PUBLISHED CONTRIBUTIONS

Recognition of the need to advance knowledge of variable ways of family members being in relationship to others has been a primary purpose of *Family Relations* editors for over three decades. Klein, Schvaneveldt, and Miller (1977) analyzed the following priorities in family study in work in progress across ninety-four projects being completed by members of NCFR during 1964–1972: theory building (through attention to developing organizing concepts into systems, i.e., structural-functional, symbolic interaction, situational and institutional frameworks); family and subsystem relationships; marriage and family formation and dissolution; transactions with other groups and or organizations; family power; sexual behavior; family life cycle; socialization; reproductive behavior; family decision-making; methodological concerns.

Family Relations also continues to add knowledge about family interaction. Between 1987–1997, dozens of articles incorporated interaction as a central topic in policy and practice areas of inquiry. The list below compiles topics that editors and reviewers believed would accomplish the journal's purpose of reporting work that could provide implications for clinical practice and interventions with family members. Contributors identified and explicated aspects of affective and social development that family members are dealing with in their interpersonal interactions with other family members and members of other institutions in society: abuse/maltreatment/violence (of parents; of children; among women; sexual abuse); addictions (including alcohol); assessment (including toddler behavior); caregiving (for elderly; for handicapped children); family diversity (including ethnic groups); family policy (collaboration of services for children and families, including custody; day care; employment; health; latchkey children; maternal employment; noncustodial parents; pregnancy prevention programs; rural services); family therapy (including family textbooks); health (AIDS; HIV); parenthood (including adolescent years; child-rearing information; divorce and stepfamilies; father's role; grandparenting; involvement of single parents in youth organizations; later life parenting; mothers and daughters; mothers, fathers, and adolescents; religious beliefs; single mothers; parenting programs (including family life education; parent education; reflective dialogue in parent education; teaching about families); resources parents use; sexuality (including intimate relationships; sexuality education); stress (and depression; and remarriage; in families); technology (including TV; computers).

The twenty-six family interaction studies identified in Table 9 offer a host of possibilities for organizing new refrains in family-institution interaction across disciplines. It is important to reiterate that the term interaction can be used in multiple ways. Table 9 is presented as just one of many possible sets of family interaction concepts based on features of the structure and organization of activities contributing directly to breaking new ground in human development (cf. Newbrough, Dokecki, Dunlop, Hogge, and Simpkins 1978). Comparing the purposes and definitions of family interaction variables presented in Table 6 and Table 7 with the Table 9 list of family study concepts provides a hint of why Head Start reviewers argued as early as 1978 that Head Start would be able to build upon ground-breaking work across disciplines in order to develop family-institution interaction concepts. Table 9 highlights a decade of efforts in representing interpersonal interactions by the National Council for Family Relations. The Table 9 summary is based upon publications from the same ten-year period that the Society for Research in Child Development disseminated the interaction research presented in Table 6 and Table 7.

Statements regarding the need to consider multiple interpretations of quality in parenting, family interaction, and family–professional institution interaction have appeared on a regular basis across *Family Relations* issues published since 1987. Quality may be just a label for displays of adult behavior that are assumed to promote self-esteem, or displays of adult behavior that are assumed to lead to a child's development of self-control, obedience, acceptance of subordinate role expectations, or lack of instances of disruptive behavior. Julian, McKenry, and McKelvey (1994) point out that practitioners should be aware of the possibility that an upbringing behavior repertoire labeled as quality may merely reflect a dominant institution's view of what is suitable or correct or appropriate to a parent. Relationship styles are much more complex than a term such as quality conveys. For example, adult-child interaction may involve "the bicultural effort of attempting to promote self esteem within one's culture and to develop competencies to deal with the harsh realities of [living in a racist society]" (p. 36).

Family Relations contributors have noted that developing knowledge of what factors need to be taken into account in family-institution interactions in terms of working with children and adults depends upon collecting information from all caregivers in the family network concerning their perceptions or interpretations of: (a) appropriate behavior (McBride 1989, 1990); (b) appropriate relationship styles (Ketterlinus, Lamb, & Nitz 1991); (c) the expectations members have of one another (Shuster 1993); (d) how parents appraise child development (Glascoe & MacLean 1990); (e) family organization and functioning differences (Visher & Visher 1989); (f) the course of structural variations in family functions (Johnston 1990); (g) the course of parenting roles and the course of engagement features of communication across stages and institutional settings of child-rearing (Pasley, Dollahite, & Ihinger-Tallman 1993; Harrist, Pettit, Dodge, & Bates 1994).

The calls for combining researcher, clinician, practitioner, and parent knowledge seem to fall into three categories:

1. continued advocacy for and demonstration of the value of subjective knowledge (i.e., rather than sole reliance on researchers' normative information) (Doescher & Sugawara, 1992),

2. continued advocacy for and demonstration of the value of understandings about the resources all individuals have for multiple interaction functions (cf. Clewell, Benasich, & Brooks-Gunn 1989), and

3. continued advocacy for and demonstration of the value of incorporating objectives related to variations within and across family social systems in family-institution interaction (e.g., preferences for interacting in a family group, or interacting in a "support group" designed by family intervention personnel) (cf. Powell, Zambrana, & Silva-Palacios 1990).

Table 9. Concepts of Family Interaction Research

Concepts Included in *Family Relations* 1987–1997	Source(s) Arranged by Year
parenting behavior repertoire and communication relationship styles	Anderson & Nuthall 1987 Harrist et al. 1994
variable family organizational patterns	Hobart 1988 Nath et al. 1991 Bronstein et al. 1993 Pasley et al. 1993
variable ways parenting functions are executed	Visher & Visher 1989 Johnston 1990 Lauer & Lauer 1991 Small & Eastman 1992
parent roles, including fathers' involvement and expectations of children	Levant et al. 1987 McBride 1989 McBride 1990
parents' appraisal of their child's development	Glascoe & MacLean 1990 Sistler & Gottfried 1990
shared child development and parent development knowledge with family members	Thomas 1996
sources of parent stress, including parenting and employment	Ketterlinus et al. 1991 Shuster 1993
variable preferences for parenting programs such as home-based intervention and center-based programs	Clewell et al. 1989 Powell et al. 1990 Doescher & Sugawara 1992
educating professionals for diversity as reflected in multicultural family studies, and child and family development textbooks	Smith & Ingoldsby 1992 Fine 1993 Julian et al. 1994 Skolnick 1997
collaboration of services for children and families	Daka-Mulwanda, Thornburg, Filbert, & Klein 1995

Source: *Family Relations* 1987–1997

In their statement of advocacy, Sistler and Gottfried (1990) propose that early childhood professionals need to remember that attempts to control the direction of adults' involvement with their children's lives will fail if their models of family functions are in disagreement with parents' cultural and generation-development knowledge.

The value of subjective knowledge is referred to repeatedly in *Family Relations* articles. In contrast to the design components reported in the empirical studies identified in Table 7, *Family Relations* articles include many examples of the usefulness of family members self-reports and family histories (e.g., Johnston 1990; Lauer & Lauer 1991). One result of this type of exploratory framework is to reach beyond a prototypical research task that expects explicit instruction from all adults in order to understand variation in norms for development across communities. "A major cultural difference may lie in the extent to which caregivers adjust their activities to children as opposed to the extent to which children are responsible for adjusting to and making sense of the adult world" (Rogoff, Mistry, Goncu, & Mosier 1993, p. 9).

Nath, Borkowski, Schellenbach, & Whitman (1991) give examples which demonstrate the value of subjective knowledge; for instance, family researchers who agree with the position that subjective knowledge is a valuable form of understanding can demonstrate that it is the individual's appraisal of support rather than a count of the sources of support, the types of support, or the amounts of support that influence mental health outcomes. The value of new understandings of interaction functions beyond controlling and regulating behaviors has also been articulated by *Family Relations* contributors Glascoe and MacLean (1990). They make the case that considering parents' interpretations of family interaction processes will help in the creation of new appraisals of development.

Contributors to *Human Development* and *Developmental Review* offer parallel streams of this idea to their readers. For example, Tappan (1989) presents a model for developing representations of subjects' family interactions based upon the meanings they communicate in narrative descriptions of their own development, and then comparing these accounts with researchers' theories of development. Following this method, his comparisons lead to the following judgment: "The correspondence (or lack thereof) between personal narrative accounts of developmental change over time and theoretical narrative accounts of development change over time is significant" (p. 310). Whereas some theories of development, such as the development of reasoning, suggest a trajectory through specific stages, Tappan did not find indications of correspondence to this tenet in his analysis of family members' answers to the question, "Do you think you respond differently to uncer-

tainty or conflict now than earlier?" After making an argument for using stories that subjects tell in answering such a question as data, Tappan recom-
mends that we consider defining development as different mixes of the
contents of theorists' assertions about the nature and substance of competence or performance.

Duncan (1991) adds another possibility for correspondence (or lack
thereof) between accounts of family interaction. Building on the work of
Parke, Power, and Gottman (1979), Patterson and Moore (1979), Minuchin
(1985), and Vuchinich (1990), Duncan identifies different perspectives on
conflict interaction held by researchers and family members. He contends
that the results of such attention will provide further knowledge of how the
child learns to accomplish behavioral regularity in interaction, as well as how
he or she deals with the meanings of such actions. He also suggests the contribution that can be made to researchers' understanding of family diversity if
attention is given to micro social-psychological processes (i.e., attention to
action taken by participants in creating, coordinating, pursuing, negotiating,
and concluding conflict).

CHAPTER THREE

Putting Selected Reviews
in Context

A s part of the strategy for locating primary family interaction research sources and perspectives that may contribute to constructing a response to the challenge that Head Start could be better, special issues devoted to family development were also identified for the 1987–1997 time frame of the SRCD and NCFR citations presented above.

The examination of special issues on family development in this chapter was conducted in terms of the light they could shed on the contention that family interaction researchers need to begin to see interaction, including verbal and nonverbal functions of language, or talk, as a means by which their own—and their subjects'—interests and assumptions are brought to light. This is not an incidental key process, but a means for examining and understanding the contexts in which subjects in a study function, and "also the contexts in which the investigator operates" (Wertsch & Youniss 1987, pp.18–19).

INTEGRATING SOCIAL AND PSYCHOLOGICAL
ASPECTS OF DEVELOPMENT

I n 1990, *Human Development* produced a special issue on efforts to integrate social and psychological aspects of development. The contents of the special issue provide specific examples of Powell's (1994) argument that "movements towards conclusive statements about the merits of particular Head Start...practices require research on program variables in context" (p. 242). Contributors began this cross-disciplinary effort in order to elaborate on both the advantages and limitations of concepts to study change. The authors provide summaries of contributions of theorists in both disciplines and attempt to identify points of convergence to foster further interest in concepts of environment, including accounts of institutional settings. Lerner and Mulkeen (1990) assert that human development is a life-span biopsychosocial phenomenon and therefore individuals need accounts to help them finds ways to critically consider the question of what influence social institutions have in optimizing their complex life-span course.

The contribution of such accounts would be twofold: both theory and practice would be enhanced. Theoretically, the accounts of the *relation* between individuals and organized contexts such as Head Start would combine ideas from multiple disciplines in order to provide explanations and obtain knowledge about how to enhance knowledge of functions. As Lerner and Mulkeen (1990) point out, repeated calls for such syntheses abound in the literature on life-span human development to accomplish purposes such as attending to the influence of social institutions in any account of human development and showing how the organized and active institutions of society provide influences on the course of human life. They characterize the outcomes of their own work in accomplishing such purposes as falling "along a success-failure continuum" (p. 180) and point out that moving across discipline knowledge is fraught with problems caused by the difficulty of communicating how functions are dynamically interactive in human life and not a set of parallel tasks. Yet they acknowledge that the difficulty of trying to communicate about context and development is offset by contributions that can be made to creating new images of "both interindividual differences in the human life course and in an individual's potential for plasticity across life" (p. 180).

In other words, Lerner and Mulkeen portray the contribution of combining ideas from multiple disciplines as enhancing knowledge of functions. Advances in knowledge occur through creating new orientations or conceptualizations that synthetically capture the concept of *relation* by inclusion of social, cognitive, and affective dimensions of interaction between individuals.

According to Nagel (1961), there has been general agreement across the social sciences since the early part of the twentieth century that accounting for how parts of a social system such as families and other institutions fit together is a promising direction for developing a comprehensive theory of social phenomena. In addition to the extent of agreement on the promise of attaining knowledge of how parts of a social system can be advanced through the use of frameworks of functional analysis of social phenomena, other promising features of decades of social science work include multiple notions of what can constitute a functional account of the interactions observed among social structures including families and other institutions. Again, developing such accounts needs to begin by restating the dilemma of multiple meanings of functional analyses and especially the problem of how to portray functioning as dynamically interactive in human life and not a set of parallel social, cognitive, and affective tasks.

Practically, accounts of *relation* would provide a means of giving voice to participants' experiences of attempts by institutions to influence their individual and social identity. As Landrine (1992) points out, the understanding of identity that dominates clinical psychology, psychiatry, and psychotherapy in the United States depends on the meanings attached and attributed to behaviors.

> People from Western culture speak of "using," "saving," "wasting," "spending," and "managing" their time; of "controlling," "regulating," and "dealing with" their emotions; of "exploiting" situations, "dealing with" interpersonal issues, "mastering" people, and "managing" others, emotions, and patients. Such colloquialisms speak to the...representation of the nonself as a lifeless and threatening object. Thus the failure to construe the nonself as lifeless and threatening..., the failure to endeavor to master and manage the nonself realm (e.g., to master situations, manage one's time, or control one's emotions) is defined as psychopathology, viz., as learned helplessness, passivity, or as deficits in social skills, self-control, and self-efficacy. (p. 403)

Answers to the common clinical query, "Tell me something about yourself," are expected to provide facts, that is, the client is expected to use colloquialisms such as the above as a means of presentation of self. Those who consider their identity as bound to social interactions, contexts, and relationships may present detailed descriptions of their interactions in specific interactions in order to characterize the various faces of identity that change from relationship to relationship. "Such stories in response to a (ostensibly) simple question about the self can be misinterpreted as circumstantial, tangential speech—a sign of underlying thought disorder [lack of intelligence, lack of "insight," or lack of verbal ability]—by therapists from Western culture" (Landrine 1992, p. 406).

Evaluating one's own work in understanding the concept of *relation* along a success-failure continuum does not only apply to coming up with ways of validating explanations of family-institution interactions that do not concentrate on describing personality characteristics. Lessons learned also apply to how one's work is also leading to identifying alternative characteristics of organizational environments. Continuing to examine whether organizational environments are complex or simple, stable or constant, changing rapidly or slowly fails to consider the impact of distrust and uncertainty on publicly funded organizations, and how uncertainty may generate opportunities and also generate defensive strategies on the part of individuals, groups, or entire organizations (Benveniste 1983). To ensure an adequate approach to the question of optimal development of individuals and their institutions, research and evaluation inquiry has to start from the premise that problems of optimizing development should be conceptualized as open...problems that have no well-defined a priori solutions" (Brandstader 1990, p. 163).

As described in the Chapter 5 discussion of interviews, the twenty-six interviews required in Head Start Standards are the occasion for considering how question-asking methods can be viewed as occasions for accomplishing factual, quantitative accountability requirements, but these evaluation occasions also have the potential for yielding useful and sensitive results about optimal development problems that have no well-defined a priori solutions. The 1990 special issue of *Human Development* on integrating study of social and psychological aspects of development anticipated how future work on problems that have no well-defined a priori solutions could lead to new orientations for developing new refrains on family-institution interaction.

Goodnow (1990) identifies two points where sociology and psychology share specific premises as well as an interest in developing accounts of optimal development within and across institutional settings:

1. The social environment influences direction through the nature of everyday practices, including face-to-face interaction, the effects of routine practices, and the dynamics of interaction between people.

2. Individuals' responses to the nature of everyday practices and routines may be displayed through a variety of interaction functions (e.g., passivity or compliance, selective acceptance, silence, resistance, rejection, or seeking information through other means).

In the same *Human Development* special issue on integrating social and psychological aspects of development, Chapman (1990) makes the point that there is no lack of models of environment or social context that can be useful in building knowledge of everyday practices and routines. The literature on contextualism and the ecology of human development is quite extensive (cf. Moen, Elder, & Luscher 1995; Wallat 1991b; Wallat & Goldman 1979). Other contributors to the special issues provide examples of advances that will proceed in the form of questions to be answered:

a. how social processes are shaped by the structure of social institutions (Chapman 1990);

b. how social processes contribute to continuity and change at varying macroecological and microecological levels, including representations of the social environment as organizational systems and interaction systems (Dannefer & Perlmutter 1990);

c. how complex formats and uses of social interaction can be identified across societies and their institutions (Fetterman & Marks 1990).

In sum, the *Human Development* special issue pointed to the need to continue trying to find ways to integrate psychological and social aspects of development. In turn, such efforts ensure moving toward advances in the analysis of the range of macro and micro levels and types of social environments and their relation to socialization effects.

In a 1990 contribution to *Merrill-Palmer Quarterly,* McCall (1990) also argues a need for incorporating concepts such as interaction styles in the continuing study of change (i.e., development). His advice is to explicate further what family members and practitioners working with families mean when they report change in patterns of attachment, aggression, or conflict.

> Techniques, especially measurement techniques, often dominate a concept, rather than the concept dominating the measurement. When a measurement or technique seems to work, everyone relies on it, it often becomes the sole measurement of that concept, and other procedures and other dependent variables are not explored.... Reliance on a single measure has the advantage of potential comparability across studies, but it also has...limitations. (p. 146)

This point was addressed further in a 1992 *Merrill-Palmer Quarterly* special issue. In her overview of the special issue on family interaction, Garvey (1992) reviews different ways that developmental psychologists may utilize the flow of talk from interviews, experimental tasks, and observational coding systems to examine aspects of socialization and language development. In the prominent paradigm found across the journals illustrated in the first part of this special publication, talk is "used as an instrument, a tool, for investigation" (p. iii). The results of using talk as an instrument or tool are presented in the form of global ratings, as when caretaking "styles are characterized as responsive or as permissive, democratic, or authoritarian" (p. iii).

Building on knowledge created during a time span that produced a dominant paradigm, developmental researchers may extend the use of interviews and experimental tasks by retaining information collected while using talk as a tool for later analysis. For example, Eisenberg (1992) observed the frequent use of justifications in children's conflicts with adults and returned to interview and observation information to ask "further questions about the antecedents, construction, or consequences of such patterns" (p. v). She was able to characterize the function of justifications in the following format of social interaction: (a) adult initiates request or action; (b) child opposes adult without providing a reason for doing so; and (c) adult solicits an accounting from the child for their action or behavior. Adoption of such strategies for using interviews and observations as a means of creating interaction material to work with has lead researchers to move beyond considering talk as just a tool. The success end of the continuum has been being able to point to a common core of interaction experiences across settings, including those relevant to family-institution interaction. Among the common core of everyday practices that are visible in collaborative social activity are functions such as formulating conflicts and justifications, and negotiating solidarity and reciprocity both in planning and enacting projects. Analysis of everyday preschool activities has brought to light the function of conflict talk in learning to negotiate and engage members of a group in a cooperative and collaborative orientation (Sheldon 1992).

What Garvey and other contributors to the *Merrill-Palmer Quarterly* special issue on talk are trying to accomplish is to demonstrate that diverse research frameworks use talk to conceptualize interaction. The success of such work is whether the concepts—or abstractions of behavior—that are inferred from the use of talk can lead to contrasting quite different images of upbringing functions and children's capabilities, such as the behavior control representations presented earlier in Table 7 and the representations of upbringing functioning presented later in this monograph in Table 10 (i.e., identity tasks, boundary tasks, managing climate, maintenance tasks, and managing system stress or participation demands). For example, there is no doubt when reading through Table 1, Head Start Performance Standards Objectives, Indicators, and Data Sources, that talk is taken into account through accomplishing the required interviews on social, cognitive, and physical development. The Head Start Standards require information about the relationship between adult-child interaction and the development of literacy. Creating compilations of findings from Head Start evaluation interviews relies on parents telling the interviewers about instances of emergent literacy, language skills, reasoning and problem solving, and social interaction with peers (Zill, Resnick & McKey 2000). Similarly, compilations of findings from Head Start evaluation interviews with staff on managing programs and involving parents in decision making (e.g., Barnes, Guerva, Garcia, Levin, & Connell 2000) are using talk as a tool to develop global categories of participation. "This is entirely appropriate for confirmatory research" (Vuchinich, Vuchinich, & Coughlin 1992, p. 72). But it means that unanswered questions about how the form and content of talk may contribute to addressing pressing policy statements, such as "Head Start could be better," are not examined.

Although "entirely appropriate" from a confirmatory standpoint, this approach also ignores insights about children that can be derived from further analysis of conversational interactions (Vuchinich, Vuchinich, & Coughlin 1992, p. 74). Once the Head Start accountability reports are done, the combinations of sayings, doings, thinkings, feelings, and valuings that are visible in parent and staff interviews should be tested against judgments of what parents and staff each consider the other should be doing. Ways of accomplishing this have been suggested in linguistics and education literature for many years (e.g., Erickson 1975b; Guilmet 1979; Gumperz 1976; Hymes 1974;). Since there is no absolute method that will tell researchers in any absolute sense all of the features of the format of social interaction used as cues by all participants, we can learn how both sides interpret and evaluate a stretch of interaction and thereby create interactive material to work with (Jupp, Roberts, & Cook-Gumperz 1982).

THE GROUNDWORK FOR FUTURE DIRECTIONS

Phillips, Voran, Kisker, Howes, and Whitebrook's (1994) policy study on child-care centers brings to a full circle what has been presented thus far. They begin their discussion of their reanalysis of data from a nationally representative survey of Head Start, public school, and community programs for infants, toddlers, and preschoolers by pointing to "increasing agreement among both researchers and policymakers that high-quality early childhood programs can ameliorate some of the negative consequences of growing up in poverty" (p. 487). Reduction of poverty provided a persuasive rationale for expanding Head Start programs in the United States during the twentieth century. Head Start exemplified the idea that inadequate preparation for schooling was one element in a series of social factors that

reinforce other social conditions, such as low-income jobs, low-quality housing, poor diet, and poor medical care. However, the need to expand knowledge about quality care, and the call to document the full range of child care
available for low-income, middle-income, and high-income families, begs the
question of whether existing levels of quality are "good enough" to become
a positive opportunity for all children. To answer questions about quality,
Phillips and her colleagues warn policymakers that they should not assume
that structural aspects of child care reported as indices of quality provide suf-
ficient information. Information on structural aspects such as group size and
ratio of adults for the number of infants, toddlers, and preschoolers receiving
care "consistently fall within the range of presumably adequate care"
(p. 482). However, information on structural aspects of teacher-child interaction—such as "harsh," "sensitive," "detached"—fail to capture the
dynamic features of children's daily experiences and interactions.

Although studies continue to identify successful educational child care
(e.g., Lazar & Darlington 1982; Campbell & Ramey 1994), they leave open
several questions about the nature of work to be done if the study of the family and larger ecological systems designed to support child and family development is approached as an interdisciplinary endeavor on human interaction
and institutional-based practices (Hareven 1971; Skolnick 1997; Zigler &
Styfco 1993).

As Hartup pointed out in his 1978 review of family interaction research,
"Failure to wed the perspectives associated with one discipline to perspectives
associated with others (e.g., developmental, biological, ecological, social systems, historical perspectives)" leads to missed opportunities and slows the
progress of the study of family interaction (Hartup 1978, p. 41).

The literature review in Chapter 2 illustrates that rethinking interaction
functions and structures—or formats of social interaction—is occurring
across fields. The questions that remain open are: What properties of interpersonal interaction that have been identified can be made explicit in studies
of contacts between family members and other institutions in the unique
ecosystem of each child (Hobbs 1979, p. 193). What properties of interpersonal interaction processes within families and other institutions can be made
explicit as attempts are made to improve developmental outcomes for children through affecting long-lasting improvements in income or socioeconomic status (Huston, McLoyd & Coll 1994, p. 281).

The possibilities for answering these questions have been laid in Head
Start Performance Standards. The set of standards, available since 1996,
require conducting parent and staff interviews as data sources for indicators
of a child's emergent literacy and language skills, motor skills, social behavior,

transition to public school institutions, and his or her access to health care. Interviews are also used to gain an understanding of connections between Head Start program goals and meeting parents' needs, and connections between program tasks and parents' influence on these tasks. In sum, the twenty-six interview data sources outlined in the Performance Standards provide a means to make explicit the interconnection across the family and Head Start as institution in accomplishing these tasks. What appears to be needed is a new starting point, or reconceptualization, of family as an institution and organizations as an institution, that would be useful in conducting these interviews in ways that can help make explicit the components of child-rearing functions across these ecological fields.

MAKING EXPLICIT INTERCONNECTIONS
ACROSS INSTITUTIONAL FUNCTIONS

As demonstrated in the literature review, family systems research and family discourse research provide conceptual and methodological resources to help build the image of how families and Head Start programs can be thought of as "analogous systems" or systems or organizations in which forms of human behavior are displayed, modified, suspended, or developed (Nagel 1961, p. 459).

Families and Head Start programs are analogous institutions with a similar key defining feature: upbringing tasks that each must accomplish regardless of variation in structure and composition. This possibility for renewing attempts to conceptualize family-institution interaction as an object of outcome assessment derives from two sources: (a) the consensus among family researchers that family functioning tasks are visible to observers of family interaction, and (b) the consensus among family communication (or institutional discourse) researchers that variation in task functioning is visible across interaction strategies used by compositions of individuals across structures or social fields.

These two starting points are displayed in Table 10. A set of five upbringing tasks identified in reviews of family research is presented in column 1 (cf. Sabatelli & Bartle 1995). Column 2 provides examples of these tasks from the work of family researchers who have attempted to make family functions explicit (cf. Duncan 1991; Glasoe & MacLean 1990; Kaye 1985). Column 3 builds on lessons learned from institutional discourse research that have

Table 10. Interconnections in Upbringing Tasks Across Institutions

INSTITUTIONAL FUNCTIONING TERMS	FAMILY AS AN UPBRINGING INSTITUTION	HEAD START AS AN UPBRINGING INSTITUTION
Identity Tasks		
Definition: Development of identity for individuals as family members and organization members is visible in communicative exchanges in which participants attempt to transmit information about qualities, attributes, strengths, and weakness. (Such information is projected into other interactions in other situations and settings.)	Variations across families in the mode (i.e., customary usage, manner or way of acting, doing, or being) adopted for executing the constellation of tasks associated with identity includes strategies (or methods and procedures) for guiding family members' interactions with others.	Organizations contain systems of meaning and action about social roles (the presentation of self) and relations. Such systems of meaning and action can be analyzed in terms of participants' assumptions about the nature of social order and control.
Boundary Tasks		
Definition: Development of external and internal boundaries occurs in order to delineate family and organization membership in the institution, and to regulate the flow of information between the institution's social fields and the social fields included in other institutions.	Patterns of distance regulation and strategies for interacting with "outsiders" in other social systems can be identified along an engagement/disengagement continuum.	Organizations contain a range of social settings that help members' structure (but not determine) conditions for responding to special interests, power, and dominance issues in predictable ways.
Managing Climate		
Definition: The development of decision-making, power, and control strategies are interconnected to varying assumptions about how conflict should operate in interaction.	Strategies associated with regulation of climate include conflict strategies.	Organizations are the setting of encounters between participants to use interactional resources to construct, sustain, and change social relationships. They can also illustrate various actions associated with the construction of quarrels, such as how the refusal to return a greeting is often associated with a distinctive participant stance or gaze.
Maintenance Tasks		
Definition: The development of the meaning of what is a resource and the development of rules about the use of these resources (i.e., resources such as time, energy, food, education).	Priorities are reflected in the implicit and explicit rules that become established about the use of resources.	Organizations provide settings to construct diverse arguments, logic, positions, and justifications for different decisions and actions on practical issues.
Managing System Stress		
Definition: The strategies (or methods and procedures) families and organizations use to determine whether change or reorganization is needed to deal with identity, boundary, climate, and maintenance tasks, introduce stress to the institution.	Dealing with changing needs and demands—whether originating from within or outside the family institution—is visible in both the stress of continuation of things as they are and the stress of challenging typical modes of interaction.	Organizational settings include attention to nondiscursive—or material—aspects of social change such as money, resources, jobs, or affordable housing. Such attention may be spent on reconstructing the frame of silence as status quo, or creating an alternative frame for silence such as resistance.

Sources: Sabatelli & Bartle (1995), G. Miller (1994)

become useful for helping practitioners interested in considering formats and functions of communication in the interactions practitioners have with clients (cf. G. Miller 1994). The examples of identity, boundary, management of climate, maintenance tasks, and managing stress identified in column 3 build on concepts and premises identified in studies of communication in institutional or organizational settings.

As the contributors to *Beyond the Blueprint: Directions for Research on Head Start's Families* (Philips & Cabrera 1996) have concluded, the need to consider the following is still apparent: How should one think about Head Start's work with families and its effects in more complex and adequate terms?

The notion of functions summarized in Table 10 provides a template for returning to earlier issues as well as considering the purpose of interviews included in Head Start Standards. In this chapter, called Putting Selected Reviews in Context, three major issues have been identified:

- finding ways to consider the question of what influences social institutions have for all participants;

- approaching the question of optimal development as open questions that have no well-defined a priori (preset) solutions;

- acknowledging that lack of attention to decades of critiques of the practices of assessment of family functioning leaves unresolved points of contention surrounding survey and interview approaches.

While worries about developing assessments that are developmentally and contextually sensitive are not new, policymakers have brought greater urgency to tackling the problem of better results. For example, family policy researchers at the University of California, Berkeley, and Yale University interviewed over 1,000 mothers using child-care centers and family–child-care homes and the providers of such care. The researchers concluded that the 1996 welfare reform law has not provided quality care for children when their mothers go to work. The staff director of the Human Resources Subcommittee of the House Ways and Means Committee stated that the researchers "have not made their case" (Jacobson 2000, p. 15). The staff director argued that the analysis of the interviews did not provide proof of long-term effects of quality care on development.

In other words, representatives of policy groups, as well as researchers studying functions of family-institution interaction, agree that it is not acceptable to draw inferences about long-term effects of quality care from displays of clinically relevant dimensions of family interaction, or schooling relevant dimensions of family talk, such as the examples presented in Table 7. The policy movement towards expanding Head Start lines up with the research imperative to dictate that it is time to use all the accumulated data, and methods for collecting it for studying development in the context of institutions interacting, instead of using discreet indicators based on individuals' performance.

Sabatelli & Bartle (1995) argue that clinical and schooling dimensions, such as control of children's social behavior and control over topics and tasks to be learned, all represent a value position: they represent a construction of what an effective family looks like through the eyes of the researcher (cf. p. 1026). Yes, they are defensible (e.g., see Purposes in Table 6) since they provide a visual representation of a dyad in which one individual attempts to control the responses of another. However, the clinical and schooling dimensions studied to date do not provide knowledge about the following aspects:

IDENTITY. What information about biophysical and psychological development of interest to clinical and school professionals gets projected into interactions with others? Is biophysical and psychological information collected in interviews considered of value to those being interviewed, and if so, how does this information serve as the foundation of individual identity, of well-being, of social identity?

BOUNDARY. What information about strategies of distance regulation can be uncovered during interviews about the use of comprehensive services and other work and non-work-related organizations in the community? Do both family and institutional members use variable interpretative frames to distance themselves from others along a continuum of engaged to disengaged? How are interaction devices for engagement and disengagement connected to the foundation of individual identity, of well-being, of social identity?

MANAGEMENT OF CLIMATE. What information about decision-making, power, and control strategies can be uncovered in the conduct of interviews?

MAINTENANCE TASKS. What, if any, resources are associated with the identification, performance, and completion of tasks?

MANAGING STRESS. What interaction strategies in developing identity, engagement and disengagement, and power and control require attention due to changing biophysical, psychological, and economic needs, demands, and tasks?

The functioning approach to family-institution interaction described above suggests that the parameters of policy analysis be enlarged, not in terms of additional techniques, but more in terms of the scope of the analysis.

CHAPTER FOUR

Reformulations of Infant, Toddler, and Preschool Care

uring the twentieth century this country witnessed an ever-increasing interest in efforts to examine what society is doing to and for children and to articulate how social institutions, including the family, determine how problems are posed, which actions can be taken, and by whom (Reich 1988). As summarized in the Appendix, the history of Head Start during the twentieth century could be turned into a story of doing policy work to create, modify, select, check, suspend, terminate, and recreate ideas about what is an environment for good, and what aspects of an environment for good are worth sustaining even if critics complain that early experiences do not necessarily ensure what will occur in the future (cf. Lewis 1997, pp. 203–204). Given what is now known about processes of doing policy work to affect change in interactions across society, the term *upbringing* will be used from this point forward to help move thinking away from separating the functions of early childhood care into separate responsibilities and towards advancing thinking towards new perspectives on interaction.

CHANGING EXPECTATIONS ABOUT FAMILY-INSTITUTION FUNCTIONING

oroney and Krysik (1998) provide a fascinating historical and contemporary analysis of changing expectations about family-institution functioning as reflected in policies and programs such as Head Start. Overall, the arguments about what *should* be done, what *can* be done, what *must* be done, and by *whom* it should be done have revolved around whether upbringing processes, including socialization, social control, nurturing, and physical and emotional care are being retained by families or being transferred to other institutions (cf. p. 142). While social scientists and policymakers continue to debate institutional arenas for *upbringing* processes, and attempt to relate these processes to responsibilities, procedures, and desired outcomes, Moroney and Krysik argue that continued use of a dichotomy (either the family *or* the state) ignores the question of how realistic our view is of upbringing functions.

"This nation over the past sixty years has evolved (although some would argue rather reluctantly) into its unique form of a modern welfare state" (Moroney & Krysik 1998, p. 49). Its uniqueness is attributed in part to a continuing debate on how individuals and families fare as economic policies are shaped to further the goals of the existing economic system. Moroney and Krysik (1998) describe policymakers' approach to families in the last seven decades of the twentieth century "as falling under two contrasting paradigms." The first, labeled the "old" paradigm, emerged during the depression of the 1930s. Provisions of programs ranging from public education to social insurance were based on a model of families at risk and under stress due to imperfect market mechanisms. "Continuing shifts in our economic system created risks and produced consequences that negatively affected the quality of family life" (p. 151). Such arguments led to social policies that were formulated to be universal in coverage.

Under the "new" paradigm adopted as the dominant ideological framework of state and national policies beginning in the 1980s, governments assumed a residual approach: "wait until the problem occurs before doing anything" (Moroney & Krysik 1998, p. 157). According to Moroney and Krysik, current selective education and benefit policies are reflected in public discourse arguments such as the following:

- Family arenas should be viewed in the same way we view economic markets, i.e., it is appropriate for the state to become involved in markets only when there is clear evidence that a market is imperfect.

- If the state becomes intrusively involved in family lives it interferes with their right to privacy and, in effect, tells families that they are not capable of meeting their own needs without outside help.

- The state should treat markets and families in similar ways. To do so otherwise permanently distorts the market and discourages families from becoming self-sufficient and independent (cf. Moroney & Krysik 1998, pp. 269–270).

Moroney and Krysik introduce the notion of bilateral exchange to expand their argument that the use of a family or state dichotomy to sort out who has what responsibility, and the use of a division of functions metaphor in public debate about families, has little practical value other than keeping expenditure down for the time being (cf. p. 157). The notion of bilateral exchange is defined as the most desirable, effective, and feasible way that family and extrafamiliar institutions relate to each other so as to maximize development.

Lewis (1997) agrees with Moroney and Krysik's view that as we move into the new millennium it seems reasonable to critique how conventional accounts of the nature of development function as continuity or discontinuity with a predictable end point have impacted our social policy and educational practices. Also calling for policy analysis to widen its scope in light of what multiple disciplines have taught us, Lewis amplifies the notion of bilateral exchanges by suggesting that the study of *Altering Fate* requires alternative frameworks or accounts for considering the complexity and unpredictability of nonrepetitive situations that affect child development on a day-to-day basis. "The model that I have argued for goes by many names, *contextualism* being just one" (Lewis 1997, p. 203). It is an account of how individuals may influence transactions between themselves and others, and how interchanges with larger economic, political, and social systems may influence institutional settings such as the home and school. According to Lewis, contextualism is a model that focuses on pragmatism (i.e., functions) and how people act currently as they attempt to adapt to situations as they find them. This requires that we focus on the contexts in which people find themselves—including interview contexts—and learn how they solve problems as they find them. This can be accomplished with an understanding that meaning-seeking functions are a part of the nature of human life. "Individuals are always adapting to their environments, and as these environments change, so do people" (Lewis 1997, p. 204). The important issue is to arrive at a realistic and reasonable picture of a major purpose of social policy.

Moroney and Krysik and Lewis's theoretical position begins with the argument that the major purpose of social policy is to create an ongoing and continuous commitment to maintaining the common good. As Lewis (1997) has stated:

> I fear that the idea of doing good for children when they are young is good for their future may not be demonstrated and that critics will continue to use this failure to withhold the time, energy, and resources necessary to do good now. What is good? It cannot be based on the future but on our sense of

what is good now for children. What children need is transparent in its simplicity (p. 204).

We should pass on to each generation the perspective that child and family researchers have articulated for the past forty years: That "the major purpose of social policies is to build the identity of persons around some community because we need to be concerned with questions of identity and alienation." (Moroney & Krysik 1998, p. 161)

COMMUNICATION: INTENTION IN POLICY AND PRACTICE

The possibility of creating communicatively competent community organizations and systems of care has been the subject of studies for many decades, and at least since the passage of the Economic Opportunity Act (EOA) in 1964 (Chernesky 1997). Evaluation of EOA centered on effectiveness as defined in four legislative provisions: (a) hiring professional staff of similar ethnic and language backgrounds as clients; (b) locating programs in communities accessible to family members; (c) designing programs so their structure and policies did not create obstacles to their use by minority groups; and (d) maximizing feasible participation.

In the three decades following implementation of EOA it became clear that "policy formulation is only about 10 percent of the challenge to realizing change, and implementation [is] the other 90 percent" (Moroney & Krysik 1998, p. 28). It has also become clear that the concepts of family participation and collaboration in the delivery of educational, health, and social services in the United States are biased in favor of "more communication." Practice and policy directions converge in agreement that "more" must be done to deal with an absent public and infuse strategies which provide opportunities and options to "maximize public participation" in the design and delivery of publicly funded programs and services (U. S. Department of Education 1993; National Endowment for the Humanities 1995).

Policies for maximizing family member participation in public forums and discussion groups portray adoption of the strategy of "more conversations" as a means to solve problems. This framing of "maximizing feasible participation" follows decades of assertions from practitioners who seek strategies to provide a voice to family members in the provision of services. Review of medical and social services trends point to a range of published assertions regarding provision of time for more talk. In his review of arguments that have been formulated since the late 1970s for involving all members of a family in assessment of services to be provided to children, Carr (1994) presents a series of case examples that demonstrate successful intervention. He ties such success to practitioners' skills in uncovering the meaning of a problem to the whole family and observing patterns of interaction that surround the presenting problem. Other medical and social service researchers (e.g., Chenail & Morris 1995; Cicourel 1987; Joanning, Demmitt, Brotherson, & Whiddon 1994; Korsch, Putnam, Frankel, & Roter 1995; Lipkin, Putnam, & Lazare 1995) have also illustrated how previously unspoken points of view can receive attention, thereby opening up possible options for family members to consider what they perceive as family problems. Such efforts directed toward identifying features of a purposeful conversation in family interviews build on ground-breaking work in creating a range of research methods to collect verbal and nonverbal material in the study of face-to-face interaction across communication contexts and penetrate patterns of social organization to investigate the invisible microinequities in the social organization of everyday institutional life (Grimshaw 1987; Gumperz 1982b; Gumperz & Cook-Gumperz 1982; Kendon, Harris, & Key 1975; G. Miller 1994; Quill 1995).

Other types of information on involvement objectives across types of services to family members are collected by the U.S. congressional General Accounting Office and other educational and social service organizations that monitor funding efforts to influence the life prospects of families and children (e.g., Finance Project 1996). Accounting audits at the federal and state level point out that parent involvement is a policy requirement in over twenty funded programs administered by the U.S. Departments of Education and Health and Human Services (Cohen 1995; U.S. General Accounting Office 1995). Parent involvement in programs such as comprehensive child development centers, family resource and support centers, and Head Start range from many hours a week to a few hours a month (U.S. General Accounting Office 1995, p. 33).

Of particular interest to congressional appropriations committee members is to identify the processes and structures associated with the program providers' levels of compliance to parent involvement requirements in funding eligibility (Knapp 1995). Advocates of family health, education, and welfare organizations seek to support such efforts to examine plausible strategies for the formulation of policy amendments, and as such, continue public funding of the delivery of educational, health, and social services to families. Such organizations call upon state-level publicly funded administrative departments, district offices, local boards, professional associations and unions, and business groups to take steps including: (a) support public review of publicly funded comprehensive services, (b) illustrate innovative practices across such services, (c) encourage development of valid measures of services provided, and (d) encourage development of a focus on results (Cohen 1995).

Across policy spheres of influence, maximizing family and community member participation are specified and required goals. For example, the U.S. Department of Health and Human Services (HHS) mandates individual family involvement in developing plans to meet educational and development needs of infants, children, or youth with disabilities (Joanning, Demmitt, Brotherson, & Whiddon 1994). Also, the U.S. General Accounting Office (GAO) has identified provision for salient speech events as a valid indicator of a program's success at linking families with a range of human services. GAO analysts argue that the common element across comprehensive services with "high levels of participation" is program deliverers who include provisions for participants and professionals to undertake the following range of speech events: (1) interviews (i.e., health, counseling), (2) committee meetings (including service providers and family members), and (3) interdisciplinary team meetings to address family members, and family problems (U.S. GAO 1993).

The GAO call for providing families with opportunities for more speech events across social, educational, and health public forums and services provides an opportunity to address whether mounting amounts of information from family members become part of the solution for further advances in efforts that are supportive of families.

These continued calls for knowledge of the nature and substance of family members' involvement in educational, medical, and other social services, and knowledge of links between providing occasions for interaction and outcome judgments of effectiveness and comprehensiveness, provide researchers with an opportunity to report their interpretations of the positive and negative aspects of broad calls for more conversation time between practitioners and clients. Scollon and Scollon's work (1980, 1981) provides examples of a careful explication of variable frames of reference on involvement.

Sociologists have noted for many years that there are consequences of information overload on social systems. A growing anomaly has become visible in advanced societies; increasing information in bureaucracies is not reducing social problems as might be plausibly expected, and information and problems are mounting hand-in-hand.

Yet the question remains of whether people could do any better with more information than they [are] doing already... Under some conditions, perfectly good information is capable of becoming noise, in the sense that it interferes with getting the information one needs. (Klapp 1978, pp. 46–47)

Sociolinguists who have developed detailed procedures to explain variability of information features across contexts and speech events such as interviews and meetings point out that significant breakdowns in communication regularly occur.

Communication cannot be studied in isolation; it must be analyzed in terms of its affect on people's lives. We must focus on what communication does: how it constrains evaluation and decision making, not merely how it is structured.....We are not separating meaning and actions in their abstract analytical form, but we are looking at how they are realized in practices and how this process of realization can influence....the relationship of the individual to public institutions. (Gumperz & Cook-Gumperz 1982, pp. 1–3)

More recently, with passage of the Americans with Disabilities Act by Congress in 1992, organizational self assessments—at both academic and service levels—have examined how organizations can take steps to modify service delivery systems to ensure that management and delivery of services are sensitive to variation and diversity in clients and providers (e.g., Aronsson & Cederborg 1996; MacPhee, Kreutzer, & Fritz 1994; Congress 1997b).

In a recent set of studies that focus primarily on issues of policy and practice relevant to work with families, Congress (1997c) points out that continual self-assessment against a set of standards such as those mandated by the Bureau of Head Start (cf. Standards Objective 5: Ensure well-managed programs that involve parents in decision making) is warranted on the basis of evidence that most practitioners are not aware that their judgments of the families they serve are rooted in their own views and visions of appropriate family roles (identity) and boundaries. Calling for further study of how practitioners' visions, beliefs, and values are translated into practice, Congress (1997a) points to Chernesky's (1997) work as an example of ways that agencies can begin to move beyond dominant orientations in the literature on appropriate, competent, and dysfunctional families. Studies of organizations' attempts to ensure that management and delivery of services are sensitive to variation and diversity have uncovered a range of microinequities that often go unnoticed or unchallenged. For example, Chernesky (1997) defines competent social service organizations such as Head Start as those continuously vigilant about conflicts that can develop due to lack of becoming conscious of the dynamics of interaction. Increased reports of conflict coincide with lack of knowledge and acknowledgment of diversity and variation in interaction styles. Chernesky further contends that biases will remain in social services with continued use of many entrenched practices that have developed on the basis of traditional views about verbal language such as those reflected in interviewing.

New images of human beings' verbal capabilities are available through concepts that have been explained in studies of formats of social interaction. Several linguistic concepts have become useful to professional practitioners interested in considering forms and features of communication in their interactions with clients and colleagues (Wallat 1991a; Wallat, Green, Conlin, & Haramis 1981: Tannen & Wallat 1993). Among concepts explicated in these attempts are: "discourses," "interpretative frames," and "style shifts." Cumulatively, the three concepts provide a new orientation to early childhood and life-span development of parents and Head Start staff. As described in the next section, the new orientation, which encompasses the work from multiple disciplines reviewed thus far, is "Learning through Discourse."

STUDIES OF DISCOURSES IN PUBLIC LIFE

The last twenty-five years have seen the development of a view of *relation* as social interactions, and views of interaction as composed of a variety of discourses of communication. In reviewing child language, socialization, and family literacy studies, it becomes apparent that each area has created knowledge that contributes to our understanding of forms and formats of talk in families and communities (Wallat 1984, 1991a). This means that new family-institution interaction studies that are designed to answer the question of performance across different ages, conditions, or settings can build upon what is currently known about language acquisition, participation in discourse settings, and language functions. Rather than starting anew, future work can use the cumulative knowledge base of past studies by adopting an orientation such as "Learning through Discourse." As diagrammed in Figure A, the cumulative work of social science disciplines on interaction serves as mutually supportive bases for addressing the question: How can we learn more about the experiences and interchanges between individuals that foster effectiveness?

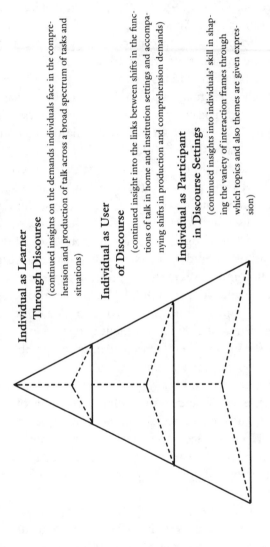

Figure A. Orientation Model for Developing Accounts
of Family-Institution Interaction:
Learning Through Discourse

Learning Through Discourse

(new insights into communicative functions
and demonstrations of ability over time and contexts)

**Individual as Learner
Through Discourse**

(continued insights on the demands individuals face in the comprehension and production of talk across a broad spectrum of tasks and
situations)

**Individual as User
of Discourse**

(continued insight into the links between shifts in the functions of talk in home and institution settings and accompa-
nying shifts in production and comprehension demands)

**Individual as Participant
in Discourse Settings**

(continued insights into individuals' skill in shaping the variety of interaction frames through
which topics and also themes are given expres-
sion)

Source: Wallat, C. (1991a). Child-adult interaction in home and community: Contributions in understanding literacy. In S. B. Silvern (Ed.), *Literacy through family, community, and school interaction* (pp. 1–36). Stamford, CT: JAI Press. Reprinted by permission of the publisher. All rights reserved.

The shape of a tetrahedron was chosen to reflect the supportive base social science disciplines provide. Unlike most models of interaction that suggest relationships between variables, the visual representation in Figure A is intended as a summary of some of the major areas of interest across disciplines that have made advances in explaining the concept of communicative competence (Wallat 1984, 1991a; Wallat & Piazza 1988). These studies are based upon perspectives reviewed thus far and are not intended to reflect the entire area of face-to-face interaction in home and organization settings. Rather the information presented in Figure A is intended to suggest what is known through providing a composite of an effective learner across anthropology, child language and psycholinguistics, social psychology, and sociology literature. The composite also suggests topics of interest across disciplines in examining what is known and unknown about human development (Wallat & Piazza 1988; 2000).

With adoption of an new orientation that considers all participants in Head Start programs as learners through discourse, users of discourse, and participants in and across discourse settings, the results of two decades of multiple discipline work on interaction in home, school, and community settings are acknowledged as common ground for study of the broad spectrum of situations covered in the twenty-six Head Start Standards interviews. The orientation model suggests the promise of viewing content across interviews from the wider lens of multiple functions of discourse. Adopting the perspective of *multiple functions* provides both a vehicle for complying with policy standards and a vehicle for identifying and explaining what dimensions of discourse suggest themselves as being comparable and worth comparative study. The cumulative work of social science disciplines diagrammed in Figure A serve as mutually supportive bases for considering the questions: What are essential and distinguishing attributes of an effective learner across the life span—i.e., individual as user of multiple discourse functions (Halliday 1973)? How do effective learners develop across the life span—i.e., individual as participant in a variety of discourse settings with a range of demands including topic confusion, topic substitution, topic rejection (Handleman 1975)?

When Cicourel (1994) points out that researchers often employ a model of questions and answers in order to make attitudes, opinions, values, and beliefs accessible for analysis of social identity or power in organizations, he indicates that there is no assurance that the content of their final reports will move beyond a count of details recorded in a large database. The problem is how to convince researchers interested in macrostudies that survey and interview material can help them accumulate insight into discourse processes and structures that constrain and facilitate responses to interview or survey questions.

> The central issue here is not so much the possibility of coding and tabulat-
> ing the frequency of turns and topics, but [developing models of] the way
> that different [cognitive, emotional, linguistic, and interactional or prag-
> matic] elements are needed to sustain the viability of the process, the
> coherency of talk, and some sense of understanding among the participants.
> (Cicourel 1994, p. 62)

While some argue that it is not up to those concerned with discourse to persuade those who are not concerned, the number of calls for combining interpretations of verbal detail with recognition of variable social meaning suggests there may be growing interest in developing a cadre of researchers capable of integrating issues of language and society in future work. Such direction would result in accumulating insight into how "some of the fea-tures and relationships obtaining in society can be grasped adequately only from the standpoint of what people mean through the ways they use lan-guage" (Hymes, 1994, p. 92). At present there are a number of scholars whose combined contributions have led to several robust concepts for con-sidering discourses in public life. The following section overviews the com-bined work of researchers across multiple disciplines. The section is organized as a glossary in order to provide an introduction to the reader on the subject of what might be learned from day-to-day attention to talk, as well as a ref-erence for later sections of the paper.

CONCEPTS FOR CONSIDERING DISCOURSES IN PUBLIC LIFE

DISCOURSE(S)

The study of discourse is part of the complex activity we loosely call "social interaction." (Cicourel 1980). It includes all forms of spoken and written text (e.g. conversations, interviews, commentaries, speeches, essays).

> The discourse from natural settings might refer to regular meetings in a
> bureaucracy, family disputes, family discussion of where to spend a vacation,
> discussions among friends about their respective lifestyles, different types of

storytelling, types of calls to a suicide prevention center, and so on....Many types of discourse analysis routinely make use of specific groups and topics as part of [a] database: For example, the study of medical interviewing, legal interviewing or courtroom cross examination, tenure assessments in academic settings, and interviewing prospective candidates for specialized jobs in government or private sectors (Cicourel 1994, pp.63–65).

Hymes (1974) made lasting contributions to laying the foundations of considering language as discourse, and developing theoretical concepts and descriptive methods that are now used to study the components of creating and reinforcing group cohesion in his classic article, "Models of the interaction of language and social life." Researchers' focus on discourse has led to descriptions of properties of interaction and formal aspects of discourse such as descriptions of properties—or forms or formats—of speech acts and variable functions of writing. Yet they cannot attribute such descriptions of properties unequivocally to things or information that are actually in the mind of participants (Cicourel 1980). The advances made by discourse researchers include the following:

- Approaches to studying discourses, including conversations and interviews, have a common concern: They stress the need to appreciate variation in meaning which emerges in talk, as well as the need to observe how this variation is used as a means of creating and reinforcing group participation and making group meanings (Hymes 1974; Lakoff 1989).

- Conversations are considered the most fundamental and pervasive means of conducting human affairs. People interact linguistically on a variety of topics in a wide range of social situations and social settings and construct, modify, or suspend a variety of norms and conventions (Wallat 1984; Wallat & Green 1982; Wallat & Piazza 1988).

- Despite this variation, conversational analysis has identified a set of characteristics that serve as a starting point for identifying contrasts in the presentation of self in conversations:

    1.   The language is often informal and inexplicit because the participants can rely on context to clarify their meaning, e.g., A: "That's a nice one." B: "It sure is."

2. While participants spontaneously construct their sentences, one can expect to hear loosely connected constructions, false starts, hesitation noises (er, um), pauses, repetitions, and other 'errors' of performance, e.g., see definition of style shifts below.

3. The concept of "conversational style" is useful in viewing the set of language features associated with personal, social, and/or occupational identity (Crystal 1987).

INTERPRETATIVE FRAMES

Individuals have configurations of expectations about how social interaction (language) and social settings should take place (e.g., taken-for-granted premises about "the way things are supposed to be" and "things that everybody knows"). Such configurations, used by individuals to come to terms with conveying information, sustaining participation, and having meaning and intent understood, are called interpretative frames. Discourses such as conversations and interviews are processes of interaction and include frames as part of their organization. Individuals scan what is going on in social settings and sort out their cognitive and social premises to help identify how much to say, what to say, and how and when to say it. Such scanning and sorting of what weight or significance to assign to stylistic shifts can be glossed as resources individuals use to combine particular instances of talk and nonverbal behaviors and construct a frame to "look" at the outline—the nature and shape—of discourses. (cf. Becker 1988; Frake 1977; Goffman 1974, 1981; Gumperz 1982a; Handleman 1975; Tannen & Wallat 1993).

For example, the phrase "developing and maintaining a level of trust and rapport with informants" describes a state of interpersonal contact and is one kind of interactive frame that can help organize a speech act such as an interview (Spencer 1994). Examining dialogues (conversations) between subject and interviewer reveals whether the two are operating with quite different ideas (interpretative frames) about the nature of the discourse in which they are engaged (e.g., Table 11). Wertsch and Youniss (1987) argue that it is inappropriate to rate subjects on a rating level for participation if researcher and subject are not using similar frames of reference (i.e. the researcher is guiding his actions holding expectations about "What is completing an interview?' and the subject is holding expectations such as "This is what I need to do to have a conversation with a stranger?").

STYLE SHIFTS

Style or stylistic shifts refer to concrete devices that make up conversational style and serve as signaling resources to convey meaning and intent. Characteristics of individual and social style have been explicated through attention to the following presentation-of-self devices:

- features of language (variable use of semantic openness, vagueness, ambiguity)

- discourse system (variable interpretative frames on when to say what and how much to say)

- grammatical system (variable interpretative frames on what to say and how to say it)

- signaling content and about content (variable meaning and intent)

Devices that have been identified as making up conversational style include:

- paralinguistic features (loudness, pitch, pauses, and tone may function as demonstration of enthusiasm through quickness of response, or use of questions);

- pacing features (e.g., overlap, timing of contribution, rate of speech, floor-getting devices such as paralinguistic features above, or echo);

- repetition features (e.g., finish another individual's statement, add to his/her line of argument, incorporate another individual's idea);

- topic cohesion features and expectations regarding diffuse topics (cf. Gumperz & Tannen 1979; Tannen 1984, 1990a, 1990b).

Using such a set of concepts that highlight advances in the study of interaction would be especially useful in further studies of interactions that take place in and across family-serving institutions such as early childhood care. In the 1994 *Child Development* special issue on family and institution contexts, Phillips, Voran, Kisker, Howes, and Whitebrook point out that available literature on early childhood settings highlights our lack of knowledge about the pressing policy issues of child care (cf. p. 478). In order to address questions of quality, examples are needed of ways to integrate accounts of daily experiences and interactions and the structural aspects of organizations in which these practices are accomplished (cf. p. 489).

Essentially, three lessons have been learned from descriptive studies conducted for the purpose of identifying instances of the theoretical concepts discourses, interpretative frames, and style shifts in face-to-face practitioner-client settings. These lessons are:

1. *Talk is not just language.* As Gee (1990) has argued, any consideration of the issue of relationships of individuals in and across social settings in which they participate, and variations in the discourses they use or encounter, is never just language. Rather, the occurrence of participation in conversations, including interviews, is essentially an example of individuals dealing with the problem of integrating "ways of acting, interacting, being, thinking, valuing, believing, gesturing, dressing, using various 'props' (books, paper, notebooks, computers, rooms, buildings, etc.) as well as using language (written or spoken)" (p. 174).

2. *Talk can be occasions of continued clashes among participants' interpretation of frames.* Sociolinguists have built on Goffman's (1974) conceptualization of frame as elements of the organization of a social interaction—and participants' subjective involvement in coming to grips with discerning what counts as information, as well as conveying information, having their meaning and intent understood, and sustaining participation. The configuration of premises individuals use to help them scan and sort out when to say, how much to say, what to say, and how to say it have been glossed as resources individuals use to construct a frame through which they combine information to look at the outline—the nature and shape of—variation in discourses (Tannen & Wallat 1982, 1983, 1986).

3. *Talk can be occasions of individual and social group variations and shifts in preferred styles for display of information.* Considerable work has been done during the last few decades to move linguistic inquiry beyond explanations of communication problems as failure to understand phonology, grammar, and lexicon. The overall conclusion from this work on the characteristics of individual and social styles is that the creation of enabling conditions

for participation cannot be accounted for as simply a matter of the "right mix" of personality traits of individuals (Gumperz & Cook-Gumperz 1982).

The term organization is used in column 3 in Table 10 to index Head Start programs as one of the two arenas of interest for the investigation of the interrelations of upbringing functioning in family-institution interaction. Following G. Miller (1994), both families and organizations such as Head Start are considered institutions in that both can be characterized through similar observable and recurring activities through which members construct, constitute, or organize relationships and social practices such as mealtimes, lessons, legal hearings, or referrals.

As illustrated in the following example of what has been learned in twenty years of study of discourse processes, the concepts of discourses, variable interpretative frames, and style shifts can be useful in identifying connections observed across individuals and social settings and explaining the phenomena of family-institution interaction as variations of features in undertaking universal interaction functions, including identity tasks, boundary tasks, managing climate, maintenance tasks, and managing stress. Scollon & Scollon's (1980, 1981) interest in identifying and illustrating interpretative practices across home, school, and community settings is the source of the following illustration of participants' variable interpretations of one universal function of interaction, which is undertaking and accomplishing tasks.

The point of presenting Table 11 is to provide a visual means of anticipating variable interpretation that can occur as individuals consider the key upbringing functions presented in Table 10. Such statements of key functions can serve as a strategy for highlighting, and eventually explaining, the ways in which different formats of social interaction are occasions in which participants work with clashes in their interpretation of frames and with variations in preferred styles for display of information about their beliefs about upbringing functions. A wealth of examples of clashes of interpretation of frames and variations in preferred styles for signaling meaning and intentions in everyday interactions are available in daily newspaper comic strips such as *Family Circle* and best-sellers such as Deborah Tannen's (1994) *Talking from 9 to 5.*

In other words, the argument underlying the presentation of Tables 10 and 11 is that because child-rearing functions are going on more or less simultaneously, those conducting required Head Start interviews can help make such functions explicit, to get them out in the open where their strengths, limitations, and implications can become visible

Table 11. Individuals as Users of Discourses-in-Public-Life

INTERPRETATIONS OF WHAT DOES NOT MAKE SENSE TO SOCIAL GROUP A SPEAKERS ABOUT GROUP B SPEAKERS (i.e., What are appropriate and inappropriate ways to accomplish identity, boundary, maintaining climate, and managing tasks.)	INTERPRETATIONS OF WHAT DOES NOT MAKE SENSE TO SOCIAL GROUP B SPEAKERS ABOUT GROUP A SPEAKERS (i.e., What are appropriate and inappropriate ways to accomplish identity, boundary, maintaining climate, and managing tasks.)
They do not speak.	They talk too much.
They keep silent.	They always talk first.
They avoid situations of talking.	They talk to strangers or people they don't know.
They only want to talk to close acquaintances.	They think they can predict the future.
They play down their own abilities.	They brag about themselves.
They act as if they expect things to be given to them.	They don't help people even when they can.
They deny planning.	They always talk about what's going to happen later.
They avoid direct questions.	They ask too many questions.
They never start a conversation.	They always interrupt.
They talk off the topic.	They only talk about what they are interested in.
They never say anything about themselves.	They don't give others a chance to talk.
They are slow to take a turn in talking.	They are always getting excited when they talk.
They ask questions in unusual places.	They talk with a flat tone of voice.
They are too indirect, inexplicit.	They aren't careful when they talk about things or people.
They don't make sense.	They just leave without saying anything.

Source: Scollon & Scollon 1980, 1981

(cf. Maxwell 1996, pp. 3–4). While sorting out assessment and practical information on these tasks from interview data sources is time-consuming, Table 11 provides a frame of reference for making researchers more alert to how they are working along a failure-success continuum in conducting interviews in order to collect explanations about upbringing tasks and talking about topics related to the nature of identity, systems of meaning across settings, and the nature of formats associated with control, power, dominance, and conflicts.

Following Alvesson (1993), the purpose of Table 10 and Table 11 is not one of method or technique, but one of conceptualization of the research object of family-institution interaction: What does it mean to "see" family-institution interaction? The idea of a unitary organizational "culture" such as families' culture or Head Start Program culture is contested: the complicated everyday interconnections or relations among and between families' and other institutions' social fields need to be kept in mind through articulating and explicating metaphors such as "cultural traffic" in contrast to "cultural islands" (Alvesson 1993, p. 118). The first step is to construct a creative and interesting interpretation of family-institution interaction: to generate an idea or insight. The second step is to describe the relationship level of participants' interests in detailed social processes such as upbringing in order to detail the scope of the claim (cf. Alversson 1993, pp. 66–67).

Maxwell (1996) and King (1994) argue that these steps do not mean that generating ideas or insights on family-institution interaction should begin from scratch. Nor do gaps in knowledge on social processes, including upbringing, mean that instruments selected by researchers to discover the compliance of Head Start programs with mandated Performance Standards miss the phenomena of interaction because of the use of preset categories. The substantial numbers of instruments now available for meeting the mandate in Head Start regulations for parent interviews provide the groundwork for clarifying and illustrating connections across family and other child-rearing institutions using types of information that we know in advance participants will be able to provide.

The point Maxwell and others such as King are trying to make is that categorizing analysis (sometimes called preset categories, or a priori categories) provides a stepping-off point for creating new knowledge about ways functioning is connected across family and organization settings. For example, one of the results of Rogoff and Toma's (1997) comparative study of shared thinking formats in interactions observed across family, community, and school settings is that the interaction format of Initiation of topics by adults (I), Responding to such initiations by children (R), and Evaluation of the child's response by the adult (E) can be observed across all three settings. As introduced earlier, and elaborated in sections to follow, Rogoff's cross-cultural work has contributed significantly to identifying universal functions of language and linguistic resources children and adults use to help construct their individual and social identity. Similarly, the measurement focus examples identified in Table 5 provide information for obtaining over fifty observation protocols included in the ACF database called *Current Head Start Research* (U.S. HHS 1999) that are available for investigating preset categories by choosing indicators of outcomes of programs on what children know and can do at the end of Head Start and how it relates to both home and classroom processes as well as family development, staff development, and community development.

Maxwell (1996) argues that laying fault on the preset categories included in instruments selected by researchers to discover compliance of Head Start programs with standards misses the point. The long-range intent of ACF in supporting such an extensive number of assessment possibilities is to encourage a new generation of researchers to learn more about the pathways to outcomes included in current standards and to help current researchers, including local program personnel, develop measurement plans using available instruments and procedures and new measures as they become available. Realization of these intentions is possible due to continued increases in funding for Head Start as well as funding of new initiatives such as Early Head Start.

Following congressional approval in 1994 for extending Head Start to serve infants and toddlers during the first three years of their life, ACF created an Early Head Start Research Consortium to monitor advances in assessing how well Early Head Start (EHS) programs implement the Head Start standards. During the first five years of EHS, over five hundred new programs were developed across the United States. The 1998 Coats Human Services Reauthorization Act provided a formula for increasing the number of programs the Head Start Bureau would be able to fund through 2003, when the next wave of reauthorization hearings were scheduled. Similar to the web site information about indicators of progress being used in Head Start research and evaluation, reports of studies being conducted to describe and analyze EHS implementation provide examples of what is currently considered state-of-the-art means for obtaining quantifiable responses and testing the generalizability of previously obtained findings, such as the results outlined in Table 7.

For example, early reports based on 510 parent interviews completed at 17 sites include results of the first round of evaluations of national and local implementation levels of EHS programs. The reports include descriptions of twenty available assessment scales used to conduct thirty interviews at each site. Topics covered through use of available preset category scales assessed knowledge of physical and mental health and development, dysfunctional parent-child interaction, stressful life events, activities associated with encouraging language development, literacy, physical development, and experiences with the outside world.

As argued throughout this monograph, building on what is known is ideally suited to examining the normative concerns of policymakers to produce outcomes in four domains:

1. child development (including health, resiliency, and social, cognitive, and language development);

2. family development (including parenting and relationships with children, the home environment and family functioning, family health, parent involvement, and economic self-sufficiency);

3. staff development (including professional development and relationships with parents);

4. community development (including enhanced child-care quality, community collaboration, and integration of services to support families with young children) (Kisker, Raikes, Boller, Pausell, Rosenberg, Coolahan, & Berlin 1999, p. 2).

The topics covered in the assessments chosen for these domains by Kisker et al. provide a base from which one can move forward to focus on variable levels of social meanings of child health and development, quality of home environment, and caregivers' relationships with parents. The question of whether parents and practitioners will view such assessments as a base that can serve as an object to develop comparisons remains unanswered.

Similar to the representations of adult-child relationships pointed out in the ten-year review of *Child Development Abstracts* journals, the prevailing conception of interaction continues to be dominated by reports of dyadic exchanges and a one-directional sequence of steps. Arguments on the advantages of a sequential, linear model or series of statements or actions made by adults and children (e.g., Table 6, Purposes of Family-Interaction Research), still appear to be more persuasive than the arguments for identifying features of variability in child and family development (e.g., special issues of *Human Development, Merrill-Palmer Quarterly,* and *Child Development*). Although the intent of the twenty-six family-institution interaction interviews included in the Head Start Performance Standards, and the eighty-plus family interviews included in the first wave of Early Head Start evaluations is to capture both linear and nonlinear elements of children's growth and development, as well as problems and personal concerns of participants in social interaction, reports based on analysis of mandated interviews still include statements describing chaotic, disorganized lives of some families and tensions among staff members. As will be elaborated upon in the Chapter 5 discussion of the nature of interviews, the lack of statements on variable levels of social meaning held by participants on clinical and educational concepts such as chaotic, disorganized, and dysfunctional may be due to overreliance on a type of interview format that uses the same asymmetrical features of discourses consistently observed in classrooms, and doctors' and counseling offices.

CHAPTER FIVE

Reconsiderations of Head Start Performance Standards

The cumulative findings from several decades of research on discourses in family and public life, and lessons learned from descriptive studies of client-practitioner interactions in organizational settings, provide several considerations for future policy evaluations, and especially future work conducted to address Sabatelli and Bartle's advice regarding developing knowledge of connections between upbringing functioning. The five dimensions of upbringing functioning described in Table 10 can serve to answer both theory and practice questions as researchers and practitioners learn how others have taught themselves to: (a) consider the *meaning* for participants of an interview situation, as well as the *meaning* that participants develop about the events, situations, and actions they are asked about in interviews, (b) take note of how participants make sense of behavior that is taking place and develop causal explanations of unanticipated phenomena and influences, and (c) reflect on how their own understandings and explanations may be related to their interactive behavior with individuals being interviewed.

The following section elaborates on the nature of interviews in research and evaluation from the perspective of researchers who have worked across family and other institutional settings. Given the current mandate included in Head Start Standards for conducting interviews, of special concern is what has been learned about the nature of interviews across social science disciplines.

CURRENT USE AND NEW POSSIBILITIES FOR INTERVIEWS

Structured interviews hold a prominent place in policy evaluation. Estimates suggest that 90 percent of all social science investigations use interview data (Briggs 1986). Circumstances including: (a) the need for a quick, descriptive, quantified account of factual information on topics known in advance, and (b) the need for testing generalizability of findings across multiple institutions are considered appropriate reasons for making interviews a routine practice that has developed since Lazarsfeld described the aims of this genre more than sixty years ago (King 1994; Lindlof 1995).

While the use of closed or short answer questions in interviews meets standard practice in policy evaluation research, question-answer formats are problematic because (a) the content of questions is the choice of the interviewer (evaluator); (b) the questions are posed to elicit responses that permit the interviewer to evaluate the interviewee's ability to infer (guess) the type of answer wanted; and (c) the questions are intended to elicit answers that fit into features of bureaucratic discourse—i.e., short phrases, explicit details, and nominalizations such as recognition, recovery, and resolution which shift verbs and adjectives into nouns and functions to make the action seem remote, static, or generalizable (cf. Wallat & Piazza 1991). As in classroom discourse and other "public sphere discourses" (Gee 1990, p. 152), the topic is initiated by the interviewer, teacher, doctor, job counselor, or administrator. When this function is enacted by only one individual in a dyad, it does not provide participants the opportunity to voice their own perspectives on the appropriateness or inappropriateness of requests for information regarding individual and social qualities (IDENTITY), how they believe family and organization opening and closing strategies (cf. Klapp 1978) may be useful ways to deal with or regulate information or situations that are perceived as damaging or irrelevant, or considered wrong in timing, amount, or subject matter (BOUNDARIES), nor how conflicts and quarrels are tied to establishing family and organization features (CLIMATE), resources (MAINTENANCE TASKS), and in-and-out-of-home actions (MANAGING STRESS).

A growing number of researchers including Alvesson (1993), Bennett (1982), Cassell and Symon (1994), Keogh (1997), Mishler (1986), and Rossman and Rallis (1998), have begun to present their reflections on what they learned they had missed when they relied in earlier work solely on interview activities ranging along a continuum from "informal" or open-ended interviews to "formal" instruments in survey research.

Alvesson (1993) cautions that the issue to pay attention to in calls for new metaphors such as upbringing functioning—or positioning practices—is not one of methods or techniques, but one of conceptualization of the research object: What can make us more alert to illuminating ways of seeing family-institution interaction? The idea of a unitary organizational culture such as family or Head Start is contested. The complicated combinations of families and other institutions in upbringing functioning suggest that thinking about fixed home and school boundaries are a researcher's construction. In upbringing functioning, institutions are not cultural islands: families and Head Start institutions are not containers of unitary subcultures. In lieu of the notion of culture or subcultures, researchers and practitioners and clients need to construct a creative and interesting insight based on decades of past work across disciplines. This requires moving beyond ending studies with accounts of ambiguity. In Alvesson's view, ambiguities are cues to diverse combinations, or configurations, but should not be the center of the analysis. Organizations are not cultural islands, but mixtures of cultural manifestations of different levels of beliefs and expectations and values about functioning. Accomplishing functions is not a matter of answering questions about the "strength" or conditions of family culture or Head Start culture. Rather, some unanswered questions are: What does the existence of cultural traffic contribute to learning formats found across home and school? How are people sorting out and assessing competing ways of talking about the same subject such as language learning? (cf. Maxwell 1996, p. 36).

For example, Rogoff and Toma (1997) recently reviewed two decades of research published on socialization and language. The particular contributions to this literature that they focused on were topics including the structure of communication dyad, and discourse structure in terms of forms of and formats for learning. In the classroom and in interactions with toddlers, teachers and parents constitute formats that demonstrate turn-taking, with children serving in turn as the other side of the dyad. It has been noted that this format holds up whether the adult is speaking to one child or a group of children. In a group situation, all of the children are expected to serve collectively as the other side of the dyad. "In this discourse, the students' (or the one child's) utterances show little indication that their ideas were in contact with those of others" (p. 485). In other words, a child's utterances were not organized in any recognizable way to extend, to refer to previous comments, or argue against ideas expressed by other students. The adult initiated all topics or questions and evaluated or tested receipt of information. Such formats of social interaction have been recorded across middle-class homes, as well as in the homes of immigrant families involved in community organizations that guide parents in carrying out academic activities with their young children. Interviews of parents with toddlers reveal reasons such as the following for asking toddlers questions that require one-word answers: Children need to be able to answer questions like that in school, so they had begun to use formats that require a child to reply to test questions such as "Where does the alligator live?" or "Look, there's an alligator, and more alligators. How many?"

Reports based on information collected to evaluate the Head Start Standards provide further examples of how people assess learning formats to match the ultimate goal of the programs, which is often called school readiness. Recent assessments of a national sample of Head Start children showed they possess academic and social skills that indicate a readiness to learn when they reach kindergarten and first grade. Head Start children make gains over the course of fall and spring in word knowledge, letter recognition, and phonemic awareness. They show minimal gains in book knowledge, and little or no change in problem behavior. Parent interviews show no increase from fall to spring in the number of parents who report reading to their children (Zill, Resnick, & McKey 2000).

Unfortunately, such reports based on evaluation of standards do not reveal other possible formats of interaction that have been observed across family and community settings. Videotapes of toddlers' interactions collected by Rogoff and Toma reveal very few test questions. In the format Rogoff and Toma refer to as building-ideas-in-a-shared-endeavor, the format of participation led by an adult is to lead and facilitate children's participation in activities, but not to fully control it to transmit information.

> For their part, many European-American parents and educators want U.S. children to be prepared for success in the increasingly collaborative arrangements that are now much more common in the workplace, and seek ways to foster children's collaborative learning along lines observed [by Rogoff in fourteen families living in the United States, Guatemala, Turkey, and India.] It seems that different communities have a great deal to learn from each other. (Rogoff & Toma 1997, p. 483)

If recordings of Head Start interviews were made available to parents and staff, they could be tested against judgments of staff and parents on activities that evaluators count as word knowledge, letter recognition, phonemic awareness, book knowledge, and problem behavior. We then might be able to address unanswered questions such as: What does the existence of cultural traffic contribute to learning formats found across home and school? How are people sorting out and assessing competing ways of talking about the same subject such as language learning?

Findings from such activities could be set-aside knowledge that is being produced through long-term efforts being publicly funded. The Early Head Start and Head Start Standards' child, family, and staff development topics are being used to measure accountability and to create a baseline for a national longitudinal study of the cognitive, social, emotional, and physical development of Head Start children (Advisory Committee on Head Start

Research and Evaluation 2000). If the interviews conducted to meet these purposes were also made available, they could be used in many ways. For example, practical guides in carrying out interviews are readily available to serve as tools for identifying comparative and contrastive features of parent and staff interviews. A wide range of computer packages created for assessing qualitative and quantitative analyses of interviews are on the market (cf. King 1994). Additionally, personal stories of how individuals learned to connect conversations and interviews about policy initiatives, including locating varying views of knowledge used by parents and practitioners, are now being published (e.g., Rossman & Rallis 1998; Congress 1997b). In contrast to House's (1979) observation that researchers, practitioners, and policy evaluators did not know what to do with 60,000 interviews collected as part of the Follow Through policy initiative, we now have a wealth of interview formats, data collection tools, and analysis technologies to handle variations of these questions: What does the existence of cultural traffic contribute to learning formats found across home and school? How are people sorting out and assessing competing ways of talking about the same subject such as language learning?

Such work is not without problems: a success-failure continuum is needed to frame such initiatives. As Mishler (1986) and others (e.g., Agar & Hobbs 1982) have cautioned: The diversity of approaches to face-to-face interaction reflects the relative newness of this direction of work in understanding human development; widely accepted, standard methods will not emerge. Nor do researchers expect "the triumph of one method as the preferred or dominant approach" to analysis of face-to-face interaction (Mishler 1986, p.142). It will remain difficult to know how much of what is said in interviews is a reflection of a belief system, "how much...is the speaker's personal interpretation, and how much is due to the interview situation itself" (Agar & Hobbs 1982, p. 1). Yet work in discourse processes and cognitive psychology has begun to characterize the structure of texts (talk and writing) in ways that will enable us to know not only who said what but also how. Through the most assessable medium—language—we will find the right retort to policymakers' judgments that Head Start could be better. Complete reports of how researchers gained access to preschool settings and job counseling settings for adults, and new images of how children and adults deal with the ambiguities, asymmetries, and attitudes that are part and parcel of formats of social interaction, are also available (e.g., Corsaro 1985; Fiksdal 1990). In continuing to do such work, "some of us have faith that we will advance our own theoretical understanding of how understanding works, and also how learning environments support language" (Heath 2000, p. 58).

In sum, the selection of literature on interviews presented above, as well as the discussion of interviews in this monograph, fit with Briggs' (1986) definition of interviews as the collection of data in face-to-face conversation situations. This consideration converges with lessons learned from several decades of work on discourses in family talk and organizational talk. As such, the references and sources chosen are those that help build the case for illuminating the meaning of actions—including silences—that occur during mandated parent and staff interviews.

We now know that interview formats can shift from causal research questions such as whether and to what extent variance in x causes variance in y, to practical causal questions such as how x plays a role in causing y, what the process is that connects x to y, or what the process is through which results are achieved. The shifts are accomplished by interviewers who are aware of different frames on uses of the term *why*. While both types of questions function to provide explanations, "they are different kinds of explanation" (Maxwell 1996, p. 58).

> When Cicourel points out that certain kinds of discourse may be unintelligible, not across class or ethnicity, merely across professions, he indicates the diversity of worlds of communication in our society, worlds which need to be grasped as a basis for use of data from them. Indeed, just as anthropologists going out to the field could, in principle, provide a cornucopia of descriptions of...speaking, merely by describing how they came to know how to ask questions, take turns, convey respect, and keep from being thrown out, so [researchers from other disciplines] attending to discourse in society could provide a picture of its many worlds of interpretation, on the basis of what their work requires them to do in any given case. (Hymes 1994, p. 90)

The following excerpts from video recordings of practice sessions at a job-training program provide a glimpse of how individuals learn to work with the problematic nature of questions and evaluative functions they perform during interviews. The videotapes were developed to elicit the trainees' interpretations and perspectives on effective and noneffective job interview strategies (cf. Akinnaso & Ajirotutu 1982; Gee 1990). *Job Interview Text 1* and *Job Interview Text 2* are from a set of twelve interviews given to students being trained for secretarial positions in public agencies and industry. The researchers (Akinnaso & Ajirotutu 1982) included these two interviews as part of their case study of speech events typical of modern bureaucratic settings. Akinnaso and Ajirotutu caution readers before presenting each interview to remember that this is recorded speech, not writing. They also point out that the material between slashes represents a set of words said with one unitary intonation, and dots represent pauses. The researchers' analysis of the two interviews is based on the judgments of all twelve students on the effective and noneffective interview strategies. The summary of judgments, labeled "evaluation," is focused on the communicative competence notion of knowing *how* and *when* to switch from ordinary conversation to "interview talk."

Job Interview Text 1

Question: Have you had any previous job experience that would demonstrate that you've shown initiative or been able to work independently?

Answer: Well / yes when I /...OK / there was this Walgreen's Agency /
I worked as a microfilm operator / OK /
And it was a snow storm /
OK / and it was usually six people / workin' in a group / uhum / and
only me and this other girl showed up /
and we had quite a lot of work to do /
and so the man / he asked us could we / you know/
do we /...do we think we could finish this work /
so me n' this girl / you know / we finished it all

Evaluation: A perfectly effective discourse is used by both participants, however, the interviewee is expected to switch from the ordinary conversation function of telling stories—or communicating a scenario that the listener can picture to a bureaucratic discourse function of specifying and explaining skills related to a job position description (Akinnaso & Ajirotutu 1982, p. 134).

Job Interview Text 2

Question: One more question was that ah, this kind of work frequently involves using your own initiative and showing sort of the ability to make independent judgment. Do you have any...can you tell me about any previous experience which you think directly show...demonstrates that you have these qualities?

Answer: Why /...well / as far as being capable of handling an office /
say if I'm left on my own / I feel I'm capable I
had a situation where one of my employers that I've been /
ah previously worked for / had to go on / a...
/ trip for say / ah three weeks and /

he was /...I was left alone to...handle the office
and run it /
And at that time / ah I didn't really have what would you say / a lot of
experience /
But I had enough experience to /...deal with any
situations that came up while he was gone /
and those that I couldn't / handle at the time /
if there was someone who had more experience than myself /
I asked questions / to find out / what procedure I would use /
So I feel I'm capable of handling just about any situation / whether it's on
my own / or under supervision

Evaluation: Both participants use a perfectly effective discourse, once again.
However, the interviewee's examples of deferring to other people's knowledge probably do not match the interviewer's meaning of "initiative" and
"independent judgment." That is, after saying she is capable of handling an
office on her own, the interviewee goes on to bring up situations that can be
evaluated as contradicting her claim (Akinnaso & Ajirotutu 1982, p. 134).

As Landrine (1992) points out, the use of traditionally accepted interview formats to collect information on how clients are meeting program
goals is problematic. An expectation that parenting should include reading to
children may not be part of the individual or social identity of all Head Start
participants. As sociolinguists point out: Many minorities do not take their
individual actions as given parameters or boundaries within which they can
create their own social identity (Gumperz & Cook-Gumperz 1982).

Thus in answer to the common clinical query, 'Tell me something about
yourself,' the client...presents a few long, detailed, concrete descriptions of
encounters and fails, from a Western perspective, to give the 'simple facts.'
...Such stories in response to a (ostensibly) simple question about the self
can be misinterpreted as circumstantial, tangential speech—a sign of....
'concrete thinking,' and so as a sign of the lack of intelligence with which
this pejorative term is associated. Thus, within the first 10 minutes of a session...Western-cultural clinicians may view the client as an unintelligent,
concrete thinker who lacks 'insight' [and] verbal ability (after all, they cannot even describe themselves)." (Landrine 1992, p. 406)

According to Gee (1990), the point to pay attention to in the above
excerpts is that interviews—similar to all discourses—signal identity and take
on the function of marking who is an insider and who is not (cf. p. 79). What
counts as important in public institutional settings "is not language, and
surely not grammar, but saying (writing)—doing—being—valuing—believ-

ing combinations" (Gee 1990, p. 142). He calls such combinations of say-ings-doings-thinkings-feelings-valuings discourses.

> Very often dominant groups in a society apply rather constant "tests" of the fluency of the dominant Discourses in which their power is symbolized; these tests become both tests of "natives" or, at least, "fluent users" of the Discourse, and *gates* to exclude "non-natives" (people whose very conflicts with dominant Discourses show they were not, in fact, "born" to them and who can often show this even when they have full mastery of a dominant Discourse on most occasions of use. The sorts of tension and conflict we have mentioned here are particularly acute when they involve tension and conflict between one's primary Discourse and a dominant secondary Discourse. (p. 158)

The two excerpts from practicing job interviews serve to illustrate that individuals are learning the features of variable public sphere discourses and how to mark that they are capable of becoming an insider in the world where the job is available. However, what is not portrayed is the tension and conflict that will almost always be present when using a dominant discourse in con-trast to the primary discourse one learns through apprenticeship in home-based practices for talking about the world. Gee concludes his discussion of tension between discourses with a question:

> Beyond changing the social structure, is there much hope? No, there is not. So we better get on about changing the social structure. Now whose job is that? I would say people who have been allocated the job of teaching. (p. 158)

The implication for Head Start Standards is that one can make various points about the use of interview discourses, but, according to Gee (1990), none of the following are, for some reason, very popular with Americans, though they seem commonplace in other countries' social theory:

1. Discourses are inherently "ideological" in the sense they crucially involve a set of values and viewpoints about the relationship between people.

2. Discourses are related to the distribution of social power and hierarchical structure in society (which is why they are always and everywhere ideological).

3. Analysis of interviews from the orientation or vantage point of social uses of discourses point out that during interviews one is

expected to speak and act, and at least appear to think and feel, in terms of the values, viewpoints, objects, and concepts put forward at the expense of others. In so doing, they will *marginalize* viewpoints and values that do not count in that discourse.

> The only problem with [these points] of view of discourses is that we should not let it obscure the equally important point that human beings can (to a certain extent) choose which discourses to be in at which times (though there is, of course, a price for these like all other choices.) And these choices are very often moral choices. (Gee 1990, p. 145)

Analysis of interviews from the orientation or vantage point of social uses of language point out that the interviewer's interest can "shift topics in a way that is disruptive to the informant, and such conditions may inhibit the informant from speaking about matters known to him or her in a language and style in which a topic is likely to appear in routine conversation" (Briggs 1986, pp. x–xi). Reports based on the use of interviews should therefore be expanded in scope to include what researchers believe they have discovered about their subjects' resources for conveying information. Researchers, staff members, and parents can review the content taken from interview records. Such records can serve as the base for discussion on the following topics by researchers, staff members, and parents: (1) What did the individual who created the interview record seem to think would count as assessment and accountability information for the funding agency? (2) What information gathering strategies seemed to be used to gather this information? (3) Would you use the same strategies to gather information? (4) What other possible strategies could be used by the interviewer to learn about upbringing tasks across home and Head Start situations?

Such commentaries included in reports will eventually lead to knowledge in three areas: (a) interviewers' developing expertise in recognizing ways that information can be conveyed, albeit in variable styles; (b) success-failure uses of available tools for identifying comparative/contrastive features of interview strategies used by both interviewers and persons interviewed; and (c) types of information that may be quite helpful in addressing public policy spokespersons' judgments that Head Start could be better.

INTERVIEWS AND THE NATURE
OF COMMUNICATIVE COMPETENCE

It is possible to expand the scope of family-institution interaction at local Head Start sites. The release of policy evaluations on the Head Start Bureau web site provide an indicator of how interviews are perceived as both a routine and unremarkable practice for locating phenomena for study and presenting findings as a neutral or objective event (cf. Mishler 1986, pp. 60–61). The findings presented in the Zill, Resnick, and McKey (2000) evaluation described above met the taken-for-granted functions of conducting interviews. However, such reports can be contrasted with reviews of adult-child interaction studies. Such reviews (e.g., Wallat 1984, 1991a; Wallat & Piazza, 1988) point out that the topics mandated in Head Start Standards for reporting growth and development (i.e., emergent literacy, language skills, numerical skills, memory, reasoning and problem solving, initiative, task mastery, social behavior and behavior problems, and social interaction with peers) do not capture a wealth of dimensions of children's competence that have been reported across disciplines. The following dimensions suggest that we now have enough information from linguistics/psycholinguistics to expect that children can have:

- an extensive knowledge of spoken words that can be conveyed in written language (they, have, guns);

- a knowledge of syntactic patterns of oral utterances ("they have guns that are shooting") and their written counterparts (they have guns);

- ability to perform a variety of speech acts (directives, assertions, requests, etc.).

From a child development perspective we can expect that children have learned:

- the concept of word,

- the concept of sentence and word order,

- the concept of story,

- an ability to focus attention on a task,

- an ability to reinterpret past experience.

These categories of analysis show: (a) the child's ability to recognize grammatical and cohesive sentences, (b) understanding of the structure of language (phonology, morphology, semantics), and (c) knowledge of some features of print. Further, the analysis categories capture the child's abilities related to storytelling, formulating main ideas, and using word categories. However, when data from interviews are analyzed from only a linguistic or developmental perspective, the complex facets of children's competence are not captured. Some facets of children's competence that can be identified by caretakers through viewing videotapes together include: use of interaction functions (e.g. negotiation, persuasion); use of routines; use of speaking styles appropriate to different occasions; use of features of various devices across settings, including tones in which messages can be delivered; use of participant strategies along a continuum of alignment from silence to topic initiator; and use of a range of persuasion strategies to present oneself to others (cf. Wallat 1991a; Wallat & Piazza 1988).

Images of children's communicative competence, such as child as persuader, as adapter, as apprentice across discourses, as social participant, as practical reasoner, as style shifter, as social problem solver, and as attention holder (cf. Wallat 1984) are built from several decades of research on multiple discourse functions visible in face-to-face interaction.

The images of children's communicative competence presented in Table 12 provide a clear example of how Head Start can demonstrate that it "can be better." Demonstrations of children's communicative competence means that Head Start data does not have to be limited to just numbers to describe how it meets an objective such as concept of word. Instead, images of children and adults' communicative competence provide a way to move beyond promises made at reauthorization hearings such as "some children know 1,000 words as 5-year-olds. Other children know 10,000 as 5-year-olds" upon arrival at kindergarten (House of Representatives June 9, 1998). Instead, images are based on studies undertaken to identify functions of language. Building on the conceptualization of language functions suggested by Halliday (1973) researchers have demonstrated that as they learn to speak, young children begin to build a system of discourse that is multifunctional. Children know what discourse is because they make use of the following multiple functions as language resources to get things done: instrumental, regulatory, interactional, personal, heuristic, imaginative, and representational or informative communication of content. These are not models of language acquisition or procedures whereby individuals learn language. "We tend to underestimate both the total extent and the functional diversity of the part played by language in the life of the child" (Halliday 1973, p. 11).

Table 12. New Images of Children's Communicative Competence

Image: Child as persuader (cf. Cook-Gumperz 1981)
Research Support: The individual's use of multiple nonverbal and paralinguistic information cues in gaining adult attention can be measured (following Snow 1979).

Image: Child as adapter (cf. Corsaro 1981)
Research Support: The individual is capable of recognizing multiple sources of information, including different social participation demands, distancing behavior demands, facial display demands, and turn-yielding demands. Individual development along these dimensions can be measured (following Ekman 1972).

Image: Child as spontaneous apprentice (cf. Miller 1977)
Research Support: The individual's ability to produce a variety of hypotheses (theories, schemes, or frames) about how something will be said or could be said can be elicited and described (following Cazden 1972).

Image: Child as craftsman (cf. Feldman 1976)
Research Support: The individual can not only identify the linguistic meaning of speech acts performed by others, but can also accept the burden of identifying the social frame and discriminating clearly between relevant and irrelevant utterances (following MacKay 1974).

Image: Child as social participant (cf. Philips 1972, 1983)
Research Support: The individual's knowledge of relations *between* people can be measured—e.g., are people strangers, or friends, or closely related (following Youniss 1975).

Image: Child as practical reasoner (cf. Cook-Gumperz 1975)
Research Support: The individual is aware of the notion that changes in behavior are demanded by different kinds of context. This awareness can be measured (following Parke 1976).

Image: Child as style-shifter (cf. Labov 1972)
Research Support: The individual has a range of skills in showing how he or she can accomplish style-shifting of some linguistic variables as the topic and social context change. Some of these skills of style-shifting can be detected qualitatively in the minor self-corrections of the speaker. Evidence from past studies point to age-related differences in the development of this dimension of communicative competence (following Labov 1972).

Image: Child as ethnographer (cf. Mishler 1972, 1979)
Research Support: The individual student as linguistic ethnographer can display a range of awareness levels to changes in linguistic context and to the social identity of the speaker. As peer tutors, children can specify what a stranger would have to know to perform any role in the class-room society (following Cazden, Cox, Dickinson, Steinberg, & Stone 1979; Mishler 1978).

Image: Child as negotiator (cf. Gumperz 1976)
Research Support: The consequences of an individual's use of multiple combinations of contextualization cues in attempting to influence a gatekeeper's decision or a teacher's performance assessment can be identified (following Mehan 1974; Erickson 1975b).

Image: Child as attention holder (cf. Sacks 1972)
Research Support: The individual can learn what terms, fine details, and/or possible descriptions can best serve as an interesting and attention-holding topic of conversation. The rules seem to be: first, learn what you are and what activities are appropriate to what you are (e.g., The baby cried. The mommy picked it up. She went to sleep.); second, learn what society expects you to be and what activities others expect of someone to whom terms refer (e.g., Sugar and spice and everything nice…that's what little girls are made of). The child's learning of social or membership categories which are deemed important b.y the adult social community in which he or she lives and the activities commonly associated with these social categories are visible in the linguistic categories used across settings (following Garnica 1979).

Gee (1990) reviews acquisition and learning interpretative frames found in social linguistics literature. An acquisition principle found in social linguistics literature is that acquisition is a process of acquiring something subconsciously by exposure to models, a process of trial and error, and practice within social groups, without formal teaching (cf. Kotulak 1999). A learning principle also articulated in social linguistics literature is that learning is a process that involves breaking down the thing to be learned by using explanation and analysis terms or through certain life experiences that trigger reflection on one's own style and the style of dominant discourses (cf. Campbell 1980; Cotterell 1995; Ostrow 1981).

Individuals know what language does because they know that language is an adaptable instrument for realizing intentions. Instrumental functions include using language to get things done, and regulatory functions that are associated with control. Interaction with other people is very obviously maintained linguistically, while personal and heuristic functions provide a range of behavioral options for asserting one's feelings and attitudes, constituting public expressions of oneself, and learning how to use language to learn (e.g., learning to recognize multiple formats of what a question is, an answer is, and what knowing or understanding can mean).

The range of meanings available through imaginative functions can range from matters of content to surrounding oneself with sounds that are not necessarily about anything at all. In contrast, representational functions are "a means of communicating about something, of expressing propositions" (Halliday 1973, p. 16). The transmission of content function is perhaps "for the child, the least important function of language: we have no way of evaluating the various functions relatively to one another" (Halliday 1973, p. 16). However, studies conducted in educational, health, and social service settings suggest that adults working in such institutional arenas primarily use this function in their interactions with others. The implication for teachers, medical professionals, job counselors, and upbringers is that considering representational language as primary, and emphasizing their use of this function in their interactions with others, falls short in recognizing the contributions others can make to interaction. This causes difficulties for others who have multiple orientations on how their intentions can be communicated.

Mainstream or dominant ways of evaluating discourse are limited. Children and adults have a repertoire of functions that can be made objects of evaluations. All speakers, by virtue of speaking, demonstrate that they know about the arrangement of and relationship among words, phrases, and clauses forming units of thought (i.e., generally called sentences). They also demonstrate that they know that language serves pragmatic or practical, efficient, and effective functions. They were not told, or did not learn, the rules for what dimensions of syntax and pragmatics go with being a member of a discourse. "No one knows them." (Gee 1990, p. xix). There is a discourse of being a first grade student or a high school student as well as a discourse of different subject matters. The combinations we say, think, feel, and do are "always indebted to the social groups to which we have been apprenticed" (p. xi). Heath (1982) suggested nearly two decades ago that this foundation serves as the base for acquiring new public discourses, including school-based literacy. However, before teachers can serve a role in apprenticing children's discourses associated with different subject matter, discourses such as interviewing, and school-based literacies must be broken down into each discourse's "myriad component skills, allowing the student to practice them repeatedly" (Gee 1990, p. 66). For example, Gee has suggested that the school-based skill known as essayist literacy is similar to the skill required for job interviews.

> Such skills involve the ability to give what-explanations, to break down verbal information into small bits of information, to notice the analytical features of items and events and to be able to recombine them in new contexts, eventually to offer reason-explanations, and finally to take meaning from [actions and] books and be able to talk about it. (p. 66)

Unfortunately, as Heath (2000) recently observed, schools and universities that prepare practitioners to work in educational settings have not made room in their curriculum for students to include methods and procedures used in the study of interactions in families and other institutions. Such change would provide substantive discipline grounding for the family and community involvement and lifelong learning requirements now appearing in Program Standards and national certification expectations for professionals. As Heath argues, the state of our knowledge about concepts of interaction dictate that the results of decades of "early-language-acquisition studies about particular [linguistic] structures and changing constructions and contexts of usage" find their way into professional development courses" (p. 56).

CONCLUDING REMARKS

There are doubts about how Head Start will be able to capture the outcomes of its institutional practices. In spite of attempts to frame clearly the importance of studying the nature and organization of

changing relations between people and their environments, interactive phenomena have been at the periphery of human development research for many
years (Lerner 1995; Thorngate 1995). However, as illustrated in this monograph, new policy regulations that require interviews of parents and staff
members provide an opportunity to return to the decades-old recommendations for attention to the functions, tasks, and processes by which individuals
and societal institutions become connected (cf. Leichter 1974, 1979).

An important next step entails examining features of interaction
processes, including staff-parent relationships, and the skills and preferences
that staff and parents bring to their experience of performing institutional
upbringing tasks across organizational settings (cf. Parker, Piotrkowski,
Kessler-Sklar, Baker, Peay, & Clark 1997, p. 19).

Accomplishing this step will require adoption of new conceptions of
family-institution interaction as occasions of two persons speaking to each
other with the potential for creating new understandings of how individuals
perceive, organize, give meaning, and express their understandings of themselves, their experiences, and their world" (Mishler 1986, p.vii). Maxwell
(1996) suggests that the strategy of listening for family and child-rearing
organization members' perspectives about attributes and strengths of development should take prominence in order to pay attention to alternative
explanations and understandings of the phenomena of family-institution
interaction.

Keogh (1997) reviews the wide range of activities variously labeled institutional ethnographies, conversational analysis, and discourse analysis that
individual researchers have constructed and modified to explore practices that
are proposed or hypothesized as actively mediating social relations between
homes and schools. She concludes that researchers may be ignoring the fact
that people already have ways of knowing the organization of the relations in
which they participate because they have their own particular versions of how
home-school communications "work." Such ways of knowing may not fit
researchers' ideas about what counts as contributions to the meaning of
parent-child-teacher relationships. However, if institutions such as home and
school are conceptualized as ongoing courses of action—what Sabatelli and
Bartle (1995) refer to as dimensions of interconnections in upbringing task
across institutions—the finding from such research advances knowledge
across social science disciplines. Such accumulations of evidence suggest that
family-institution interaction must be viewed as ongoing courses of action
that intersect with other political and class relations. The locus of institutional
interaction study must therefore shift to an untouched terrain of inquiry: the
study of the work, or positioning practices, that parents, children, and teach-

ers get done at the interface of institutional encounters between representatives of each institution.

Family-institution interaction is a study, in the broadest sense, of the problem of articulation. Its aim is to shed light on the ways environmental conditions, including demographics, politics, and economics, may be changing and the ways institutional contexts are gaining access to resources based on these conditions, or are confronting the limitations of such environmental conditions (cf. Wuthnow 1989). The endeavor to use family-institution interaction data is not without risk. First, miscommunication is a ubiquitous feature of everyday practices—indeed everyday life—and routines in settings designed to interact with family members (Coupland, Wiemann, & Giles 1991; Grimshaw 1994; Linnell & Luckmann 1991; J. Miller 1994; Ochs 1991). Second, and perhaps the biggest hurdle to overcome in policy studies based on interaction, is the acknowledgment by policy evaluation and analysis researchers that they do not know what to do with the information collected. As early as 1979, House pointed out that researchers acknowledged not knowing what to do with information collected during 60,000 interviews of parents with children in intervention programs because they were considered too personalistic. More recently, critics of the current state of the study of information used across the social sciences have admitted that methods for analysis of face-to-face interactions across institutions have become bogged down in descriptions of registers such as "motherese" and "teacher talk" in instructional settings such as small group, and peer conferences on writing. However, the influence of four decades of accumulated knowledge of how language works, and how content, language and socialization matter, could materialize in the twenty-first century, as new researchers and practitioners act on the advice to pay attention to what has been learned in these topics and combine it with what is being learned about strategy building and planful thinking in other disciplines such as cognitive psychology. Investigations of discourses of varying origins and purposes such as newspapers, descriptions of organizations, and funding guidelines—now available on web sites—provide opportunities to collect evidence of long-term development of children and adult discourses used to show reasoning (i.e., syntax structures for arguing a point or debating an issue using variable criteria of what counts as "correct" in a newspaper, organization, and bureaucratic discourse) (Heath 2000: Goldman 1997).

The growing availability of researchers' reflections on how they learned to ask questions beyond a routine or standard interview format has led to a reformulation of interviewing as a means of developing knowledge of "central questions in the social and behavioral sciences, namely how individuals perceive, organize, give meaning to, and express their understandings of themselves, their experiences, and their worlds" (Mishler 1986, p. vii). New perspectives on the nature of discourse in institutional systems such as family service institutions can lead to completion of studies that provide a range of approaches for considering interaction phenomenon across social fields, and ways of using family members' conversations, interactions, or speech acts, such as interviews, to represent the situation of child and family development. Future reviews of how practitioners build on this new "ground-breaking" work will give a more precise indication of where processes of articulation of new refrains in family-institution functioning may be taking place.

Head Start: A Historical Perspective 1965–2000

President Lyndon B. Johnson (1963–1969)

January 1964
President Johnson declares "War on Poverty" in his State of the Union address.

Jan–Feb 1964
Sargent Shriver is named head of War on Poverty program by President Johnson. He convenes first task force meeting to plan legislation.

July–August 1964
July 1964. Economic Opportunity Act passes Senate.
August 1964. Economic Opportunity Act passes House and is signed into law.

December 1964
Shriver asks Dr. Robert Cooke, pediatrician at Johns Hopkins University, to head a steering committee of specialists in all fields to discuss what should be done for young children.

January 1965
Sterring committee convenes at the White House led by Lady Bird Johnson and Sargent Shriver.

February 1965
Recommendations for the Head Start program are issued by the planning committee in the Cooke Memorandum. OEO memo from Jules Sugarman announces initiation of Head Start.

May 18, 1965
President Lyndon B. Johnson officially announces the Head Start program in the White House Rose Garden.

Summer 1965
Head Start is launched, serving over 560,000 children and families across America in an eight-week summer program.

President Richard M. Nixon (1969–1974)

1969
Head Start is transferred from the Office of Economic Opportunity to the Department of Health, Education and Welfare and becomes part of HEW's Office of Child Development.

1972
Economic Opportunity Act is amended, calling for expansion of Head Start program opportunities for handicapped children. The Legislation mandates that at least 10 percent of the national enrollment of Head Start consist of handicapped children.

1973
Head Start home-based program option is added.

President Gerald R. Ford (1974–1977)

1974
Total number of children served since 1965 reaches 5,300,000.

1975
Head Start Program performance standards are issued.

President Jimmy Carter (1977–1981)

1977
Bilingual and bicultural Head Start migrant programs serve 6,000 children in 21 states.

1977–1981
Major expansion of Head Start, adding 43,000 children and families.

President Ronald Reagan (1981–1989)

1984
Head Start budget exceeds the one billion dollar mark and the number of children served since the beginning reaches 9,144,990.

President George Herbert Walker Bush (1989–1993)

1992
Head Start funding is increased by $600 million. This additional funding extends services to another 180,000 children and families.

President William Jefferson Clinton (1993–2001)

1995	1996	1998	2000
First Early Head Start grants are awarded to provide services for children birth to age three and pregnant women.	First major revision of the Head Start program performance standards is issued.	Head Start Reauthorization Act includes mandate to fund national research on the impact of Head Start.	Head Start celebrates thirty-fifth anniversary and marks the creation of 16,000 Head Start centers in its thirty-five-year history.

Notes

CHAPTER ONE: INTRODUCTION

1. In their review of ACYF family research supported studies, Newbrough, Dokecki, Dunlop, Hogge, and Simpkins (1978) suggested that "the study of family-institutional interactions are the newest and latest investigated aspects of ACYF's research agenda" (p. 55). They traced the roots of this conceptualization of family research to the growing interest in interaction as reciprocal influence with adults engaged in mediating variables in attempts to affect the child's ideas, valuations, and assessment. Such interests are viewed as an alternative to the majority of research efforts throughout this century that fall into the "one-way effect category" (p. 56). One-way effect research "concentrates on (a) families' perceptions of and attitudes toward institutions or (b) the effects upon family life of institutional policies, practices, and procedures viewed from the unilateral perspective of institutional initiatives....[and (c) on] studies in which parents are 'trained' or oriented'—projects that imply one-way communication and in which efforts on parents often are viewed as intervening variables related to child outcomes" (p. 56).

CHAPTER TWO: LITERATURE REVIEW

1. An overview of the development of ecological perspectives in considering family-institution interaction can be found in Wallat and Goldman 1979.
2. A larger sample of 985 mothers of infants is participating in the Infant Health and Development Program (Yogman, Kindlon, & Earls 1995).

Observations of father interaction during play with their 12, 24 and 36-month-old children will also be analyzed in the project.

3. The "theory and methodology" search also led to seven comprehensive reviews of over 1,000 interaction coding schemes, rating scales, and survey and interview schedules developed across the sixty-five-year period 1929–1996 to measure mother-child interaction, family phenomena, and child behavior change (Grant 1994; Grotevant & Carlson 1989; Lindholm & Touliatos 1993; Munson 1996; Sabatelli & Bartle 1995; Schwartz & Olswang 1996; Stafford & Bayer 1993).

Bibliography

Advisory Committee on Head Start Research and Evaluation. (2000). *Head Start family and child experiences survey (FACES)*. Washington, DC: U.S. Department of Health and Human Services, Head Start Bureau. Retrieved from www2.acf.dhhs.gov/programs/hsb/hsreac/faces/index.

Agar, M. & J. R. Hobbs. (1982). Interpreting discourse: Coherence and the analysis of ethnographic interviews. *Discourse Processes* 5(1): 1–32.

Akinnaso, F. N. & C. S. Ajirotutu. (1982). Performance and ethnic style in job interviews. In J. J. Gumperz. Ed. *Language and social identity*, 119–144. New York, NY: Cambridge University Press.

Alvesson, M. (1993). *Cultural perspectives on organizations*. New York, NY: Cambridge University Press.

Alvey, C. L. & S. R. Aeschleman. (1990). Evaluation of a parent training program for teaching mentally retarded children age-appropriate restaurant skills: A preliminary investigation. *Journal of Mental Deficiency Research* 34: 421–428.

Anderson, S. & P. Nuthall. (1987). Parent communication training across three stages of child rearing. *Family Relations* 36(1): 40–44.

Aronsson, K. & A. Cederborg (1996). Coming of age in family therapy talk: Perspective setting in multiparty problem formulation. *Discourse Processes* 21: 191–211.

Baird, S. M., L. Haas, K. McCormick, C. Carruth, & K. D. Turner. (1992). Approaching an objective system for observation and measurement: Infant-Parent Social Interaction Code. *Topics in Early Childhood Special Education* 12: 544–571.

Barkley, R. A. (1988). The effects of methyiphenidate on the interactions of preschool ADHD children with their mothers. *Journal of the American Academy of Child and Adolescent Psychiatry* 27: 336–341.

Barkley, R. A. (1989). Hyperactive girls and boys: Stimulant drug effects on mother-child interactions. *Journal of Child Psychology and Psychiatry* 30: 379–390.

Barnes, H. V., M. D. Guerva, G. Garcia, M. Levin, & D. B. Connell. (2000). *How do Head Start staff characteristics relate to parent involvement and satisfaction?* Washington, DC: Department of Health and Human Services. Advisory Committee on Head Start Research and Evaluation. Retrieved from www2. acf.dhhs.gov/programs/hsb/ hsreac/faces.

Becker, A. L. (1988). Language in particular: A lecture. In D. Tannen. Ed. *Linguistics in context: Connecting observation and understanding,* 17–35. Stamford, CT: Ablex.

Becker, G. & C. Becker. (1994). The Maternal Behavior Inventory: Measuring the behavioral side of mother-infant attachment. *Social Behavior and Personality* 22(2): 177–194.

Beckwith, L. (1988). Intervention with disadvantaged parents of sick preterm infants. *Psychiatry* 51: 242–247.

Benasich, A. A., J. Brooks-Gunn, & B. C. Clewell. (1992). How do mothers benefit from early intervention programs? *Journal of Applied Developmental Psychology* 13: 311–362.

Bennett, A. (1982). Strategies and counterstrategies in the use of yes-no questions in discourse. In J. J. Gumperz. Ed. *Language and social identity,* 95–107. New York, NY: Cambridge University Press.

Benveniste, G. (1983). *Bureaucracy.* San Francisco, CA: Boyd and Fraser.

Birkel, R. C., R. M. Lerner, & M. A. Smyer. (1989). Applied developmental psychology as an implementation of a life-span view of human development. *Journal of Applied Developmental Psychology* 11: 425–445.

Bornstein, M. H., ed. (1995). *Handbook of parenting.* Volume 1, Children and parenting; Volume 2, Biology and ecology of parenting; Volume 3, Status and social conditions of parenting; Volume 4, Applied and practical parenting. Mahwah, NJ: Lawrence Erlbaum.

Bradley, R. H. & B. M. Caldwell. (1995). Caregiving and the regulation of child growth and development: Describing proximal aspects of caregiving systems. *Developmental Review* 15: 38–85.

Brandtstader, J. (1990). Commentary: Special issue on sociological perspectives on human development. *Human Development* 33: 160–164.

Briggs, C. L. (1986). *Learning how to ask: A sociolinguistic appraisal of the role of the interview in social science research.* New York, NY: Cambridge University Press.

Bronstein, P., J. Clauson, J. Frankel, M. Stoll, & C. Abrams. (1993). Parenting behavior and children's social, psychological, and academic adjustment in diverse family structures. *Family Relations* 42(3): 268–276.

Campbell, S. B., A. M. Breaux, L. J. Ewing, E. K. Szumowski, & W. W. Pierce. (1987). Parent-identified problem preschoolers: Mother-child interaction during play at intake and 1 year follow up. *Journal of Abnormal Child Psychology* 14: 425–440.

Campbell, F. A. & C. T. Ramey. (1994). Effects of early intervention on intellectual and academic achievement: A follow-up study of children from low-income families. *Child Development* 65 (2): 684–698.

Campbell, B. M. (July 16, 1980). If you ask me: Ain't misbehaving. *Washington Post,* p. B5.

Campbell, R. L. & M. H. Bickhard. (1992). Types of constraints on development: An interactivist approach. *Developmental Review* 12: 311–338.

Carnegie Corporation of New York. (1996). *Years of promise: A comprehensive learning strategy for America's children.* New York, NY: Carnegie Corporation.

Carr, A. (1994). Involving children in family therapy and systematic consultation. *Journal of Family Psychotherapy* 5(1): 41–59.

Cassell, C. & G. Symon, eds. (1994). *Qualitative methods in organizational research: A practical guide.* Thousand Oaks, CA: Sage.

Cazden, C. B. (1972). *Language in early childhood education.* Washington, DC: National Association for the Education of Young Children.

Cazden, C. B., M. Cox, D. Dickinson, Z. Steinberg, & C. Stone. (1979). "You all gonna hafta listen": Peer teaching in a primary classroom. In W. A. Collins. Ed. *Children's language and communication,* 183–231. Mahaw, NJ: Lawrence Erlbaum.

Cerezo, M. A., A. D'Ocon, & L. Dolz. (1996). Mother-child interactive patterns in abusive families versus nonabusive families: An observational study. *Child Abuse and Neglect* 20(7): 573–587.

Chapman, M. (1990). Commentary. *Human Development* 33: 165–168.

Chatoor, I., J. Egan, P. Getson, E. Menvielle, & A. O'Donnell. (1988). Mother-infant interactions in infantile anorexia nervosa. *Journal of the American Academy of Child and Adolescent Psychiatry* 27: 535–540.

Chenail, R. J. & G. H. Morris. (1995). Introduction: The talk of the clinic. In G. H. Morris & R. J. Chenail. Eds. *The talk of the clinic: Explorations in the analysis of medical and therapeutic discourse,* 1–15. Mahwah, NJ: Lawrence Erlbaum.

Chernesky, R. H. (1997). Managing agencies for multicultural services. In E. P. Congress. Ed. *Multicultural perspectives in working with families,* 17–33. New York, NY: Springer.

Cicourel, A. V. (1980). Three models of discourse analysis: The role of social structure. *Discourse Processes* 3 (2): 101–132.

Cicourel, A. V. (1987). The interpenetration of communicative contexts: Examples from medical encounters. *Social Psychology Quarterly* 50(2): 217–226.

Cicourel, A. V. (1994). Theoretical and methodological suggestions for using discourse to recreate aspects of social structure. In A. D. Grimshaw. Ed. *What's going on here? Complementary studies of professional talk,* Vol. 43, *Advances in discourse processes,* 61–89. Stamford, CT: Ablex.

Clark-Stewart, A. (1977). *Child care in the family: A review of research and some propositions for policy.* New York, NY: Academic Press.

Clewell, B., A. Benasich, & J. Brooks-Gunn. (1989). Evaluating child related outcomes of parenting programs. *Family Relations* 38(2): 201–209.

Cohen, D. L. (October 11, 1995). Collaborative services face an uncertain future. *Education Week* 14(32): 19, 23.

Congress, E. P. (1997a). Conclusion: Ethical issues and future directions. In E. P. Congress. Ed. *Multicultural perspectives in working with families,* 333–338. New York, NY: Springer.

Congress, E. P. (1997b). Preface. In E. P. Congress. Ed. *Multicultural perspectives in working with families,* xvii–xxv. New York, NY: Springer.

Congress, E. P. (1997c). Using the culturagram to assess and empower culturally diverse families. In E. P. Congress. Ed. *Multicultural perspectives in working with families,* 3–16. New York, NY: Springer.

Congressional Research Service. (2001). *Head Start: Background and funding.* Washington, DC: Congressional Research Service, Library of Congress (CRS Report for Congress RS20537, January 10, 2001). Retrieved from http://usinfo.state.gov/usa/infousa/educ.

Cook-Gumperz, J. (1975). The child as practical reasoner. In B. Blount & M. Sanchez. Eds. *Sociocultural dimensions of language use,* 137–162. New York, NY: Academic Press.

Cook-Gumperz, J. (1981). Persuasive talk: The social organization of children's talk. In J. L. Green and C. Wallat. Eds. *Ethnography and language in educational settings,* 25–50. Stamford, CT: Ablex.

Cook-Gumperz, J. (1995). Rethinking testing in a diverse society. *Discourse Processes* 19(1): 165–169.

Cooper, H. M. (1982). Scientific guidelines for conducting integrative research reviews. *Review of Educational Research* 52(2): 291–302.

Coplin, J. W. & A. C. Hlouts. (1991). Father involvement in parent training for oppositional child behavior: Progress or stagnation? *Child and Family Behavior Therapy* 13: 29–51.

Corsaro, W. A. (1981). Entering the child's world: Research strategies for field entry and data collection. In J. L. Green & C. Wallat. Eds. *Ethnography and language in educational settings,* 117–146. Stamford, CT: Ablex.

Corsaro, W. A. (1985). *Friendship and peer culture in the early years.* Stamford, CT: Ablex.

Cotterell, B. (December 7, 1995). Politics: Don't lie, and stress the message. *Tallahassee Democrat,* p. 8C.

Coupland, N., J. M. Wiemann, & H. Giles. (1991). Talk as "problem" and communication as "miscommunication": An integrative analysis. In N. Coupland, H. Giles, & J. M. Wiemann. Eds. *"Miscommunication" and problematic talk,* 1–17. Thousand Oaks, CA: Sage.

Cramer, B., & D. N. Stern. (1988). Evaluation of changes in mother-infant brief psychotherapy. *Infant Mental Health Journal* 9: 20–45.

Crystal, D. (1987). The Cambridge encyclopedia of language. New York, NY: Cambridge University Press.

Daka-Mulwanda, V., K. B. Thornburg, L. Filbert, & T. Klein. (1995). Collaboration of services for children and families: A synthesis of recent research and recommendations. *Family Relations* 44(2): 219–223.

Dannefer, D. & M. Perlmutter. (1990). Development as a multidimensional process: Individual and social constituents. *Human Development* 33: 108–137.

DiLalla, D. L. & P. M. Crittenden. (1990). Dimensions of maltreated children's home behavior: A factor analysis approach. *Infant Behavior and Development* 13: 439–460.

Doescher, S., & A. Sugawara. (1992). Impact of prosocial home and school-based interventions on preschool children's cooperative behavior. *Family Relations* 41(2): 200–204.

Doise, W. (1990). Commentary: Special issue on sociological perspectives on human development. *Human Development* 33: 169–170.

Dror, Y. (1970). Prolegomenon to policy sciences. *Policy Sciences* 1: 135–150.

Drotar, D., D. Eckerle, J. Satola, J. Pallotta, & B. Wyatt. (1990). Maternal interactional behavior with nonorganic failure-to-thrive infants: A case comparison study. *Child Abuse and Neglect* 14: 41–51.

Dumas, J. E., J. A. Gibson, & J. B. Albin. (1989a). Behavioral correlates of maternal depressive symptomatology in conduct-disorder children. *Journal of Consulting and Clinical Psychology* 57: 516–521.

Dumas, J. E. & J. C. Lechowicz. (1989b). When do noncompliant children comply? Implications for family behavior therapy. *Child and Family Behavior Therapy* 11: 21–38.

Duncan, S. (1991). Convention and conflict in the child's interaction with others. *Developmental Review* 11: 337–367.

Edwards, A. D. & D. P. C. Westgate. (1994). *Investigating classroom talk.* Philadelphia, PA: Falmer.

Eisenberg, N. (Fall, 1992). Social development: Current trends and future possibilities. *Society for Research in Child Development Newsletter* 1: 10–11.

Eisenhart, M. (1998). On the subject of interpretive reviews. *Review of Educational Research* 68(4): 391–399.

Ekman, P. (1972). Universals and cultural differences in facial expressions of emotions. In J. K. Cole. Ed. *Nebraska Symposium on Motivations* Vol. 19, 207–284. Lincoln: University of Nebraska Press.

Emde, R. N. (1994). Individuality, context, and the search for meaning. *Child Development* 65: 719–737.

Entwisle, D. R. & N. M. Astone. (1994). Some practical guidelines for measuring youth's race/ethnicity and socioeconomic status. *Child Development* 65: 1521–1540.

Erickson, F. (1975a). Afterthoughts. In A. Kendon, R. M. Harris, & M. R. Key. Eds. *Organization of behavior in face to face interaction,* 483–485. Chicago, IL: Mouton.

Erickson, F. (1975b). Gatekeeping and the melting pot: Interaction in counseling encounters. *Harvard Educational Review* 45(1): 44–70.

Eyberg, S. (1988). Parent-child interaction therapy: Integration of traditional and behavioral concerns. *Child and Family Behavior Therapy* 10: 33–46.

Feldman, D. H. (1976). The child as craftsman. *Phi Delta Kappan* 58(1): 143–149.

Fetterman, D. L. & N. F. Marks. (1990). Commentary: special issue on sociological perspectives on human development. *Human Development* 33: 171–178.

Fiksdal, S. (1990). *The right time and pace: A microanalysis of cross-cultural gatekeeping interviews.* Stamford, CT: Ablex.

Finance Project. (1996). *Building strong communities: Crafting a legislative foundation.* Washington, DC: Finance Project.

Fine, M. A. (1993). Current approaches to understanding family diversity: An overview of the special issue. *Family Relations* 42(3): 235–237.

Fischer, F. (1998). Beyond empiricism: Post inquiry in postpositivist perspective. *Policy Studies Journal* 26: 129–146.

Floyd, F. J. & K. A. Phillippe. (1993). Parental interactions with children with and without mental retardation: Behavior management, coerciveness, and positive exchange. *American Journal on Mental Retardation* 97(6): 673–684.

Frake, C. O. (1977). Plying frames can be dangerous: Some reflections on methodology in cognitive anthropology. *Quarterly Newsletter of the Institute for Comparative Human Development* 1(3): 1–7. New York, NY: The Rockefeller University.

Furstenberg, F. F. (1985). Sociological ventures in child development. *Child Development* 56(2): 281–288.

Gardner, F. E. M. (1987). Positive interaction between mothers and conduct-problem children: Is there training for harmony as well as fighting? *Journal of Abnormal Child Psychology* 15: 263–293.

Garnica, O. K. (1979). The boys have the muscles and the girls have the sexy legs: Adult-child speech and the use of generic person labels. In O. K. Garnica & M. L. King. Eds. *Language, children and society,* 135–148. New York, NY: Pergamon Press.

Garvey, C. (1992). Introduction: Special issue on talk. *Merrill-Palmer Quarterly* 38(1): iii–vii.

Gauvain, M. (Winter, 1997). Observations of developmental psychologists at home. *Society for Research in Child Development SRCD Newsletter* 40(1): 3, 8–9.

Gee, J. (1990). *Social linguistics and literacies: Ideology in Discourses.* Philadelphia, PA: Falmer.

Glascoe, F., & W. MacLean. (1990). How parents appraise their child's development. *Family Relations* 39(3): 280–283.

Goffman, E. (1974). *Frame analysis.* New York, NY: Harper & Row.

Goffman, E. (1981). *Forms of talk.* Philadelphia, PA: University of Pennsylvania Press.

Gold, M., ed. (1999). *The complete social scientist: A Kurt Lewin reader.* Washington, DC: American Psychological Association.

Goldman, S. (1997). Learning from text: Reflections on 20 years of research and suggestions for new directions of inquiry. *Discourse Processes* 23(3): 357–398.

Goodnow, J. J. (1990). Using sociology to extend psychological accounts of cognitive development. *Human Development* 33: 81–107.

Grant, V. T. (1994). Sex of infant differences in mother-infant interaction: A reinterpretation of past findings. *Developmental Review* 14: 1–26.

Graue, M. E. (1993). Expectations and ideas coming to school. *Early Childhood Research Quarterly* 8: 53–73.

Grimshaw, A. D. (1987). Disambiguating discourse: Members' skill and analysts' problem. *Social Psychology Quarterly* 50(2): 186–204.

Grotevant, H. D. & C. I. Carlson. (1989). *Family assessment: A guide to methods and measures.* New York, NY: Guilford Press.

Guilmet, G. M. (1979). Maternal perception of urban Navajo and Caucasian children's classroom behavior. *Human Organization* 38(1): 87–91.

Gumperz, J. J. (1976). Language, communication and public negotiation. In P. Sanday. Ed. *Anthropology and the public interest,* 273–292. New York, NY: Academic Press.

Gumperz, J. J. (1982a). Discourse strategies. New York, NY: Cambridge University Press.

Gumperz, J. J., ed. (1982b). *Language and social identity.* New York, NY: Cambridge University Press.

Gumperz, J. J. & J. Cook-Gumperz. (1982). Introduction: Language and the communication of social identity. In J. J. Gumperz. Ed. *Language and social identity,* 1–21. New York, NY: Cambridge University Press.

Gumperz, J. J. & D. Tannen. (1979). Individual and social differences in language use. In C. F. Fillmore. Ed. *Individual differences in language ability and language behavior,* 305–325. New York, NY: Academic Press.

Halliday, M. A. K. (1973). *Explorations in the functions of language.* London: Edward Arnold.

Hamilton, E. B., C. Hammen, G. Minasian, & M. Jones. (1993). Communication styles of children of mothers with affective disorders, chronic medical illness, and normal controls: A contextual perspective. *Journal of Abnormal Child Psychology* 21(1): 51–63.

Handelman, D. (1975). Domains of definition in interaction. In A. Kendon, R. M. Harris, & M. R. Kay. Eds. *Organization of behavior in face to face interaction,* 477–481. Chicago, IL: Mouton.

Hareven, T. K. (1971). The history of the family as an interdisciplinary field. *Journal of Interdisciplinary History* 2: 399–414.

Harris, J. R. (1995). Where is the child's environment? A group socialization theory of development. *Psychological Review* 102(3): 458–489.

Harrist, A. W., G. S. Pettit, K. A. Dodge, & J. E. Bates. (1994). Dyadic synchrony in mother-child interaction: Relations with children's subsequent kindergarten adjustment. *Family Relations* 43(4): 417–424.

Hartup, W. W. (1978). Perspectives on child and family interaction: Past, present, and future. In R. M. Lerner & G. B. Spanier. Eds. *Child influences on marital and family interaction: A life-span perspective*, 23–46. New York, NY: Academic Press.

Hauser, R. M. (1994). Measuring socioeconomic status in studies of child development. *Child Development*, 65, 1541–1545.

Hauser-Cram, P. & M. W. Krauss. (1991). Measuring change in children and families. *Journal of Early Intervention* 15(3): 288–297.

Haynes-Seman, C. (1987). Developmental origins of moral masochism: a failure-to-thrive toddlers' interactions with mother. *Child Abuse & Neglect* 11: 319–330.

Heath, S. B. (1982). *Way with words: Language, life, and work in communities and classrooms*. New York, NY: Cambridge University Press.

Heath, S. B. (2000). Linguistics in the study of Language in Education. *Harvard Educational Review* 70(1): 49–59.

Hecht, B. F., H. G. Levine, & A. B. Mastergeorge. (1993). Conversational roles of children with developmental delays and their mothers in natural and semi-structured situations. *American Journal of Mental Retardation* 97: 419–429.

Heermann, J. A., L. Colette Jones, & R. L. Wikoff. (1994). Measurement of parent behavior during interactions with their infants. *Infant Behavior and Development* 17: 311–321.

Hobart, C. (1988). Perception of parent-child relationships in first married and remarried families. *Family Relations* 37(2): 175–182.

Hobbs, N. (1979). Families, schools, and communities: An ecosystem for children. In H. J. Leichter. Ed. *Families and communities as educators*, 192–202. New York, NY: Teachers College Press.

Hoffman, Y. & Drotar, D. (1991). The impact of postpartum depressed mood on mother-infant interaction: Like mother like baby? *Infant Mental Health Journal* 12: 65–80.

House, E. R. (1979) The objectivity, fairness, and justice of federal evaluation policy as reflected in the Follow Through evaluation. *Educational Evaluation and Policy Analysis* 1(1): 28–42.

House of Representatives. (June 9, 1998). *Committee on Education and the Workforce Head Start Reauthorization Hearings before the Subcommittee on Early Childhood, Youth and Families* 105th Congress, 2nd Session. [Statement of Dr. Catherine Snow, Chair, Human Development and Psychology, Harvard Graduate School of Education]. Washington, D.C.: House of Representatives (Serial No. 105–114) Retrieved from http://commdocs.house.gov/ committees/edu/hedcewS-114.000.

Howlin, P., & M. Rutter (1989). Mothers' speech to autistic children; A preliminary causal analysis. *Journal of Child Psychology and Psychiatry* 30: 819–843.

Huston, A. C. (1994). Children in poverty: Designing research to affect policy. *Social Policy Report Society for Research in Child Development* 7(2): 1–12.

Huston, A. C., V. C. McLoyd, & C. G. Coll. (1994). Children and poverty: Issues in contemporary research. *Child Development* 65(2): 275–282.

Hymes, D. (1994). Discussion: Theoretical and methodological suggestions for using discourse to recreate aspects of social structure. In A. D. Grimshaw. Ed. *What's going on here? Complementary studies of professional talk,* Vol. 43, *Advances in Discourse Processes,* 89–94. Stamford, CT: Ablex.

Hymes, D. (1974). Models of the interaction of language and social life. In J. J. Gumperz & D. Hymes. Eds. *Directions in sociolinguistics,* 35–71. New York, NY: Holt, Rinehart & Winston.

Jackson, G. B. (1980). Methods for integrative reviews. *Review of Educational Research* 50(3): 438–460.

Jacobson, L. (April 28, 1999). Head Start works, but it could be better, research shows. *Education Week* 18(33): 8.

Jacobson, L. (February 9, 2000). Problems in child care found to persist. *Education Week* 19(22): 1, 15.

Joanning, H., A. Demmitt, M. J. Brotherson, & D. Whiddon. (1994). The individualized family service plan: A growth area for family therapy. *Journal of Family Psychotherapy* 5(3): 69–81.

Johnston, C. & W. E. Pelham Jr. (1990). Maternal characteristics, rating of child behavior, and mother-child interactions in families and children with externalizing disorders. *Journal of Abnormal Child Psychiatry* 16: 45–56.

Johnston, J. (1990). Role diffusion and role reversal: Structural variations in divorced families and children's functioning. *Family Relations* 39(4): 405–413.

Julian, T. W., P. C. McKenry, & M. W. McKelvey. (1994). Cultural variations in parenting: Perceptions of Caucasian, African-American, Hispanic, and Asian-American parents. *Family Relations* 43(1): 30–37.

Jupp, T. C., C. Roberts, & J. Cook-Gumperz. (1982). Language and disadvantage: The hidden process. In J. J. Gumperz. Ed. *Language and social identity,* 232–256. New York, NY: Cambridge University Press.

Kasari, C., S. Freeman, P. Mundy, & M. D. Sigman. (1995). Attention regulation by children with Down Syndrome: Coordinated joint attention and social referencing looks. *American Journal on Mental Retardation* 100(2): 128–136.

Kasari, C., M. Sigman, P. Mundy, & N. Yirmiya. (1988). Caregiver interaction with autistic children. *Journal of Abnormal Child Psychology* 16:45–56.

Kaye, K. (1985). Family Development. *Child Development* 56(2): 279–280.

Kendon, A., R. M. Harris, & M. R. Key. Eds. *Organization of behavior in face to face interaction.* Paris, The Hague: Mouton Publishers. [Distributed in the U.S. by Aldine, Chicago].

Keogh, J. (1997). Pronouns as positioning practices in home-school communications. *Lingusitics and Education* 9(1): 1–23.

Ketterlinus, R., M. Lamb, & K. Nitz. (1991). Developmental and ecological sources of stress among adolescent parents. *Family Relations* 40(4): 435–441.

King, N. (1994). The qualitative research interview. In C. Cassell & G. Symon. Eds. *Qualitative methods in organizational research,* 14–36. Thousand Oaks, CA: Sage.

Kisker, E. E., H. Raikes, K. Boller, D. Paulsell, L. Rosenberg, K. Coolahan, & L. J. Berlin. (1999). *Leading the way: Characteristics and early experiences of selected Early Head Start programs* (Contract No. HHS-105-95-1936). Washington, D.C.: U. S. Department of Health and Human Services, Administration on Children, Youth and Families. Retrieved from www.mathematica-mpr.com/leadexec; www.mathematica-mpr.com/leadvol1; www.mathematica-mpr.com/leadvol2.

Klapp, O. E. (1978). *Opening and closing: Strategies of information adaptation in society.* New York, NY: Cambridge University Press.

Klein, D. M., J. D. Schvaneveldt, & B. C. Miller. (1977). The attitudes and activities of contemporary family theorists. *Journal of Comparative Family Studies* 8(1): 5–27.

Knapp, M. S. (1995). How shall we study comprehensive, collaborative services for children and families? *Educational Researcher* 24(4): 5–16.

Koester, L. S. (1995). Face-to-face interactions between hearing mothers and their deaf or hearing infants. *Infant Behavior and Development* 18: 145–153.

Konstantareas, M. M., H. Kajdeman, S. Homatidis, & A. McCabe. (1988). Maternal speech to verbal and higher functioning versus nonverbal and lower functioning autistic children. *Journal of Autism and Development Disorders* 18: 647–656.

Korsch, B., S. M. Putnam, R. M. Frankel, & D. Roter. (1995). An overview of research on medical interviewing. In M. Lipkin, S. M. Putnam, & A. Lazare. Eds. *The medical interview: Clinical care, education, and research,* 475–481. New York, NY: Springer-Verlag.

Kotulak, R. (January 11, 1999). Making sense of it all starts early. *Tallahassee Democrat,* p. 6C.

Labov, W. (1972). *Sociolinguistic patterns.* Philadelphia, PA: University of Pennsylvania Press.

Lakoff, R. (1989). The way we were; or, the real actual truth about generative semantics. *Journal of Pragmatics* 13: 939–988.

Lamb, M. E. (1979). Issues in the study of social interaction: An introduction. In M. E. Lamb, S. J. Suomi, & G. R. Stephenson. Eds. *Social interaction analysiss,* 1–10. Madison, WI: University of Wisconsin Press.

Landrine, H. (1992). Clinical implications of cultural differences: The referential versus the indexical self. *Clinical Psychology Review* 12: 401–415.

Laosa, L. (1989). Social competence in childhood: Toward a developmental sociocultural relativistic paradigm. *Journal of Applied Developmental Psychiatry* 10: 447–468.

Lasswell, H. (1970). The emerging conception of the policy sciences. *Policy Sciences* 1: 3–14.

Lauer, J. & R. Lauer. (1991). The long-term relational consequences of problematic family backgrounds. *Family Relations* 40(3): 286–290.

Lawes, R. (1999). Marriage: An analysis of discourse. *British Journal of Sociology* 38: 1–20.

Lawton, M. (October 25, 1995). Schools face fiscal, social impact of medical cuts. *Education Week* 14(32): 27, 30.

Lazar, I. & R. Darlington. (1982). Lasting effects of early education. *Monographs of the Society for Research in Child Development* 47(2–3): Serial No. 195.

Leichter, H. J., ed. (1974). *The family as educator.* New York, NY: Teachers College Press.

Leichter, H. J., ed. (1979). *Families and communities as educators.* New York, NY: Teachers College Press.

Lerner, R. M. (1995). Developing individuals within changing contexts: Implications of developmental contextualism for human development research, policy and programs. In T. A. Kindermann & J. Valsiner. Eds. *Development of person-context relations,* 13–38. Mahwah, NJ: Lawrence Erlbaum.

Lerner, R. M. & P. Mulkeen. (1990). Commentary: Special issue on sociological perspectives on human development. *Human Development* 33: 179–184.

Levant, R., J. Loiselle, & S. Slattery. (1987). Father's involvement in housework and child care with daughters. *Family Relations* 36(2): 152–157.

Lewis, M., ed. (1984). *Beyond the dyad.* New York, NY: Plenum Press.

Lewis, M. (1991). Ways of knowing: Objective self-awareness or consciousness. *Developmental Review* 11: 231–243.

Lewis, M. (1997). *Altering fate: Why the past does not predict the future.* New York, NY: Guilford.

Lindlof, T. R. (1995). *Qualitative communication research methods.* Thousand Oaks, CA: Sage.

Lindholm, B. W. & J. Touliatos. (1993). Measurement trends in family research. *Psychological Reports* 72: 1265–1266.

Linnell, P. & T. Luckmann. (1991). Asymmetries in dialogue: Some conceptual preliminaries. In I. Markova & K. Foppa. Eds. *Asymmetries in dialogue,* 1–20. Hertfordshire, England: Harvester Wheatsheaf. [Available from Savage, MD: Barnes and Noble].

Lipkin, M., S. M. Putnam, & A. Lazare, eds. (1995). *The medical interview: Clinical care, education, and research.* New York, NY: Springer-Verlag.

MacKay, R. (1974). Standardized tests: Objective/objectified measures of "competence." In A. V. Cicourel et al. Eds. *Language use and school performance,* 218–247. New York, NY: Academic Press.

MacPhee, D., J. C. Kreutzer, & J. J. Fritz. (1994). Infusing a diversity perspective into human development courses. *Child Development* 65(2): 699–715.

Marsiglio, W. (1993). Contemporary scholarship on fatherhood. *Journal of Family Issues* 14(4): 484–509.

Maxwell, J. A. (1996). *Qualitative research design.* Thousand Oaks, CA: Sage.

McBride, B. A. (1989). Stress and fathers' parental competence: Implications for family life and parent educators. *Family Relations* 38(4): 385–389.

McBride, B. A. (1990). The effects of a parent education/playgroup program on father involvement in child rearing. *Family Relations* 39(3): 250–256.

McCall, R. B. (1990). Infancy research: Individual differences. *Merrill-Palmer Quarterly* 36: 141–158.

McGraw, K. O. (1991). The empirical interests of developmental psychology. *Merrill-Palmer Quarterly* 37(2): 209–230.

Mehan, H. (1974). Accomplishing classroom lessons. In A. V. Cicourcel et al. Eds. *Language use and school performance,* 76–142. New York, NY: Academic Press.

Miller, G. (1994). Toward ethnographies of institutional discourse: Proposal and suggestions. *Journal of Contemporary Ethnography* 23(3): 280–306.

Miller, G. A. (1977). *Spontaneous apprentices: Children and language.* New York, NY: Seabury Press.

Miller, J. (1994). A family's sense of power in their community: Theoretical and research issues. *Smith College Studies in Social Work* 64(3): 221–243.

Minuchin, P. (1985). Families and individual development: Provocations from the field of family therapy. *Child Development* 56(2): 289–302.

Mishler, E. G. (1972). Implications of teacher strategies for language and cognition: Observations in first-grade classrooms. In C. B. Cazden, V. P. John, & D. Hymes. Eds. *Functions of language in the classroom,* 267–289. New York, NY: Teachers College Press.

Mishler, E. G. (1978). Studies in dialogue and discourse: III. Utterance structure and utterance function in interrogative sequences. *Journal of Psycholinguistic Research* 7: 279–305.

Mishler, E. G. (1979). Would you trade cookies for popcorn: Talk of trade among six-year-old children. In O. K. Garnica & M. L. King. Eds. *Language, children and society,* 221–236. New York, NY: Pergamon Press.

Mishler, E. G. (1986). *Research interviewing: Context and narrative.* Cambridge, MA: Harvard University Press.

Moen, P., G. Elder, & K. Luscher. (Eds.). (1995). *Examining lives in context: Perspectives on the ecology of human development.* Washington, DC: American Psychological Association.

Moroney, R. M. & J. Krysik. (1998). *Social policy and social work: Critical essays on the welfare state.* New York, NY: Aldine De Gruyter.

Munson, L. J. (1996). Review of rating scales that measure parent-infant interaction. *Topics in Early Childhood Special Education* 16(1): 1–25.

Nagel, E. (1961). *The structure of science: Problems in the logic of scientific explanations.* New York, NY: Harcourt, Brace & World.

Nath, P., J. Borkowski, C. Schellenbach, & T. Whitman. (1991). Understanding adolescent parenting: The dimensions and functions of social support. *Family Relations* 40(3): 411–420.

National Endowment for the Humanities. (1995). *National conversation newsletter: Fall 1995.* Washington, DC: National Endowment for the Humanities.

Newbrough, J. R., P. R. Dokecki, K. H. Dunlop, J. H. Hogge, & C. G. Simpkins. (1978). *Families and family-institution transactions in child development.* (Contract No. 105-77-1045). Washington, DC: Administration for Children, Youth, and Families.

Ochs, E. (1979). Transcription as theory. In E. Ochs & B. Schefflin. Eds. *Developmental pragmatics,* 43–72. New York, NY: Academic Press.

Ochs, E. (1991). Misunderstanding children. In N. Coupland, H. Giles & J. M. Wiemann. Eds. *"Miscommunication" and problematic talk,* 44–60. Thousand Oaks, CA: Sage.

Olson, S. L., J. E. Bates, & K. Bayles. (1990). Early antecedents of childhood impulsivity: The role of parent-child interaction, cognitive competence, and temperament. *Journal of Abnormal Child Psychology* 18: 317–334.

Ostrow, J. (August 10, 1981). High-tech speech coaches: Now you can watch what you say. *Washington Post,* Business Section, p. 21.

Parke, R. D. (1976). Social cues, social control and ecological validity. *Merrill-Palmer Quarterly* 22: 111–123.

Parke, R. D., T. G. Power, & J. M. Gottman. (1979). Conceptualizing and quantifying influence patterns in the family. In M. S. Lamb. Ed. *Social interaction analysis: Methodological issues,* 231–252. Madison, WI: University of Wisconsin Press.

Parker, F. L., C. S. Piotrkowski, S. Kessler-Sklar, A. J. L. Baker, L. Peay, & B. Clark. (1997). *Final Report: Parent involvement in Head Start.* New York, NY: National Council of Jewish Women. Retrieved from cpmcnet.columbia.edu/dept/sph/popfam/pubs.

Pasley, K., D. Dollahite, & M. Ihinger-Tallman. (1993). Bridging the gap: Clinical applications of research findings on the spouse and stepparent roles in remarriage. *Family Relations* 42(3): 15–32.

Patterson, G. R. & D. Moore. (1979). Interactive patterns as units of behavior. In M. E. Lamb. Ed. *Social interaction: Methodological issues* 77–96. Madison, WI: University of Wisconsin Press.

Phares, V. (1996). Conducting nonsexist research, prevention, and treatment with fathers and mothers. *Psychology of Women Quarterly* 20: 55–77.

Philips, S. U. (1972). Participant structures and communicative competence. In C. B. Cazden, V. P. Hohn, & D. Hymes. Eds. *Functions of language in the classroom,* 370–394. New York, NY: Teachers College Press.

Philips, S. U. (1983). *The invisible culture.* New York, NY: Longman.

Phillips, D. A. & N. J. Cabrera, eds. (1996). *Beyond the blueprint: Directions for research on Head Start Families.* Washington, DC: National Academy Press. Retrieved from http://ericps.uiuc.edu/nccic/research/nrc_bynd/notice.

Phillips, D. A., M. Voran, E. Kisker, C. Howes, & M. Whitebrook. (1994). Child care for children in poverty: Opportunity or inequity. *Child Development* 65(2): 472–492.

Pianta, R .C., B. Egeland, & A. Hyatt. (1987). Maternal relationship history as an indicator of development risk. *American Journal of Orthopsychiatry* 56: 385–398.

Polansky, N. A., J. M. Gaudin, & A. C. Kilpatrick. (1992). The Maternal Characteristics Scale: A cross validation. *Child Welfare* LXXI(3): 271–279.

Powell, D. R. (1994). Head Start and research: Notes on a special issue. *Early Childhood Research Quarterly* 9: 241–242.

Powell, D. R., R. Zambrana, & V. Silva-Palacios. (1990). Designing culturally responsive parent programs: A comparison of low-income Mexican and Mexican-American mothers' preferences. *Family Relations* 39(3): 298–304.

Quill, T. E. (1995). Barriers to effective communication. In M. Lipkin, S. M. Putnam, & A. Lazare. Eds. *The medical interview: Clinical care, education, and research,* 110–121. New York, NY: Springer-Verlag.

Reese, H. W. (1993). Developments in child psychology from the 1960s to the 1990s. *Developmental Review* 13: 503–524.

Reich, R. R. (1988). *The power of public ideas.* Cambridge, MA: Ballinger.

Rogoff, B., J. Mistry, A. Goncu, & C. Mosier. (1993). Guided participation in cultural activity by toddlers and caregivers. *Monographs of the Society for Research in Child Development* 58(8): 1–183.

Rogoff, B. & C. Toma. (1997). Shared thinking: Community and institutional variations. *Discourse Processes* 23(3): 471–497.

Rossman, G. B. & S. F. Rallis. (1998). *Learning in the field: An introduction to qualitative research.* Thousand Oaks, CA: Sage.

Rutter, M. & E. Schopler. (1992). Classification of pervasive developmental disorders: Some concepts and practical considerations. *Journal of Autism and Developmental Disorders* 22(4): 459–482.

Sabatelli, R. M. & S. E. Bartle. (1995). Survey approaches to the assessment of family functioning: Conceptual, operational, and analytical issues. *Journal of Marriage and the Family* 57: 1025–1039.

Sabatelli, R. M. & R. J. Waldron. (1995). Measurement issues in the assessment of the experiences of parenthood. *Journal of Marriage and the Family* 57: 969–980.

Sacks, H. (1972). On the analyzability of stories by children. In J. Gumperz and D. Hymes. Eds. *Directions in sociolinguistics,* 325–345. New York, NY: Holt, Rinehart & Winston.

Schwandt, T. A. (1998). The interpretative review of educational matters: Is there any other kind? *Review of Educational Research* 68(4): 409–412.

Schwartz, I. S. & L. B. Olswang. (1996). Evaluating child behavior change in natural settings: Exploring alternative strategies for data collection. *Topics in Early Childhood Special Education* 16(1): 82–101.

Scollon, R. & S. B. K. Scollon. (1980). *Athabaskan-english and interethnic communication*. Fairbanks, AL: University of Alaska, Center for Cross-Cultural Studies.

Scollon, R. & S. B. K. Scollon. (1981). *Narrative, literacy and face in interethnic communication*. Stamford, CT: Ablex.

Searle, J. R. (1969). *Speech acts*. New York, NY: Cambridge University Press.

Shapiro, T., E. Frosch, & S. Arnold. (1987). Communication interactions between mothers and their autistic children: Application of a new instrument and changes after treatment. *Journal of the American Academy of Child and Adolescent Psychiatry* 26, 485–490.

Sheldon, A. (1992). Conflict talk: sociolinguistic challenges to self-assertion and how young girls meet them. *Merrill-Palmer Quarterly* 38(1): 95–117.

Shuster, C. (1993). Employed first-time mothers: A typology of maternal responses to integrating parenting and employment. *Family Relations* 42(3): 13–20.

Sistler, A. & N. Gottfried. (1990). Shared child development knowledge between grandmother and mother. *Family Relations* 37(2): 175–182.

Skolnick, A. (1997). The battle of the textbooks: Bringing in cultural wars. *Family Relations* 46(3): 219–222.

Small, S., & C. Eastman. (1992). A conceptual framework for understanding the responsibilities and needs of parents. *Family Relations* 40(4): 455–462.

Smith, S. & B. Ingoldsby. (1992). Multicultural family studies: Educating students for diversity. *Family Relations* 41(1): 25-30.

Snow, C. E. (1979). The role of social interaction in language acquisition. In W.A. Collins. Ed. *Children's language and communication: The 12th Annual Minnesota Symposium on Child Psychology*, 157–182. Mahwah, NJ: Lawrence Erlbaum.

Spencer, J. W. (1994). Mutual relevance of ethnography and discourse. *Journal of Contemporary Ethnography* 23(3): 267–279.

Stafford, L. & C. L. Bayer. (1993). *Interaction between parents and children*. Thousand Oaks, CA: Sage.

Steele, C. & C. Wallat. (March, 1997). Welfare reform: The positioning of academic work. *Qualitative Report* 3(1): 1–8. Retrieved from www. nova.edu/ssss/QR/QR3-1/wallat.html.

Strayhorn, J. M. & C. S. Weidman. (1989). Reduction of attention deficit and internalizing symptoms in preschoolers through parent-child interaction training. *Journal of the American Academy of Child and Adolescent Psychiatry* 28(6): 888–896.

Sugland, B. W., M. Zaslow, C. Blumenthal, K. A. Moore, J. R. Smith, J. Brooks-Gunn, T. J. Griffin, D. Coates, & R. Bradley. (1995). The Early Childhood HOME Inventory and HOME-Short Form in differing racial/ethnic groups. *Journal of Family Issues* 16(5): 632–663.

Tannen, D. (1984). *Conversational style: Analyzing talk among friends.* Stamford, CT: Ablex.

Tannen, D. (1990a). Editor's Introduction: Special issue on gender and conversational interaction. *Discourse Processes* 13(1): 1–4.

Tannen, D. (1990b). *You just don't understand: Women and men in conversation.* New York, NY: William Morrow.

Tannen, D. (1994). *Talking from 9 to 5: Women and men in the workplace.* New York, NY: William Morrow.

Tannen, D. & C. Wallat. (1982). A sociolinguistic analysis of multiple demands on the pediatrician in doctor/mother/child interaction. In R. DiPietro. Ed. *Linguistics and the professions,* 39–50. Stamford, CT: Ablex.

Tannen, D. & C. Wallat. (1983). Doctor/mother/child communication: Linguistic analysis of a pediatric examination. In S. Fisher & A. D. Todd. Eds. *The social organization of doctor/patient communication,* 203–219. New York, NY: Center for Applied Linguistics Harcourt Brace Jovanovich.

Tannen, D. & C. Wallat. (1986). Medical professionals and parents: A linguistic analysis of communication across contexts. *Language and Society* 15: 295–312.

Tannen, D. & C. Wallat. (1993). Interactive frames and knowledge schemas in interaction. In D. Tannen. Ed. *Framing in discourse,* 57–76. New York, NY: Oxford University Press.

Tappan, M. B. (1989). Stories lived and stories told: The narrative structure of moral development. *Human Development* 32: 300–315.

Teachman, J. D. (1995). Families as natural experiments: A procedure for estimating the potentially biasing influence of families on relationships between variables. *Journal of Family Issues* 16(5): 519–537.

Thomas, R. (1996). Reflective dialogue parent education designs: Focus on parent development. *Family Relations* 45(2): 189–200.

Thorngate, W. (1995). Accounting for person-context relations and their development. In T. A. Kindermann & J. Valsiner. Eds. (1995). *Development of person-context relations,* 39–54. Mahwah, NJ: Lawrence Erlbaum.

U.S. Department of Education. (1993). *Guide to developing educational partnerships.* Washington, DC: U.S. Government Printing Office: (U.S. Government Printing Office: 1993-300-808-814/93170).

U.S. Department of Health and Human Services. (October 27, 1998). *(Fact Sheet) Improving Head Start: A success story.* Washington, DC. Retrieved from www.hhs.gov/news/press/1998press/981027.

U.S. Department of Health and Human Services. Administration for Children and Families. Administration for Children, Youth and Families. (April 1999). *Head Start performance measures progress report.* Washington, DC. Retrieved from www2.acf.dhhs.gov/programs/ hsb/text_only_html.

U.S. General Accounting Office. (1993). *School-linked human services.* Washington, DC: U.S. General Accounting Office. (GAO/HRD 94-21).

U.S. General Accounting Office. (1995). *Early Childhood programs: Multiple programs and target groups.* Washington, DC: U.S. General Accounting Office. (GAO/HEHS 95-4FS).

Visher, E. & J. Visher. (1989). Parenting coalitions after marriage: Dynamics and therapeutic guidelines. *Family Relations* 38(1): 65–70.

Vuchinich, S. (1990). The sequential organization of closing in verbal family conflict. In A. D. Grimshaw. Ed. *Conflict-talk: Sociolinguistic investigations of arguments in conversations,* 118–138. Cambridge, MA: Cambridge University Press.

Vuchinich, S., R. Vuchinich, & C. Coughlin. (1992). Family talk and parent-child relationships: Toward integrating deductive and inductive paradigms. *Merrill-Palmer Quarterly* 38: 69–93.

Wallat, C. (1984). An overview of communicative competence. In C. Rivera. Ed. *Communicative competence approaches to language proficiency assessment: Research and application,* 2–33. Bristol, PA: Taylor & Francis.

Wallat, C. (1991a). Child-adult interaction in home and community: Contributions in understanding literacy. In S. B. Silvern. Ed. *Literacy through family, community, and school interaction,* 1–36. Stamford, CT: JAI Press.

Wallat, C. (April, 1991b). *The concept of 'social context' as reflected in new OFRI Centers.* Paper presented at the meeting of the American Educational Research Association, Chicago, IL. Reproduced by American Institutes for Research, ERIC Clearinghouse on Tests, Measurement, and Evaluation. Educational research directions 1990–1995; Extracts from descriptions of primary tasks of OERI Centers from March 1990 RFP and 17 winning proposals. (ERIC Document Reproduction Service No. ED 408 366).

Wallat, C. & R. Goldman. (1979). *Home/school/community interaction: What we know and why we don't know more.* Columbus, OH: Merrill.

Wallat, C. & J. Green. (1982). Construction of social norms by teachers and children: The first year of school. In K. M. Borman. Ed. *The social life of children in a changing society,* 97–122. Mahwah, NJ: Lawrence Erlbaum.

Wallat, C., J. L. Green, S. M. Conlin, & M. Haramis. (1981). Issues related to action research in the classroom—The teacher and researcher as a team. In J. L. Green & C. Wallat. Eds. *Ethnography and language in educational settings,* 87–116. Stamford, CT: Ablex.

Wallat, C. & C. Piazza. (1988). The classroom and beyond: Issues in the analysis of multiple studies of communicative competence. In J. Green & J. Harker. Eds. *Multiple perspective analyses of discourse processes.* Vol. 28. *Advances in discourse processes,* 309–341. Stamford, CT: Ablex.

Wallat, C. & C. Piazza. (1991). Perspectives on production of written educational policy reports. *Journal of Education Policy* 6(1): 63–84.

Wallat, C. & C. Piazza. (1997). Early childhood evaluation and policy analysis: A communicative framework for the next decade. *Journal of Education Policy Analysis Archives* 15(5): 1–45. Retrieved from http//epaa.asu.edu/epaa.

Wallat, C. & C. Piazza. (2000). Critical examinations of the known and unknown in social science: Where do we go from here? *Qualitative Report* 5(1&2): 1–27. Retrieved from http//www.nova.edu/ssss/ QR.

Wallat, C. & C. I. Steele. (1999). Facing the consequences: Identifying the limitations of how we categorize people in research and policy. *Education Policy Analysis Archives* 7(21): 1–24. Retrieved from http//epaa.asu.edu/epaa.

Webster-Stratton, C. (1988). Mothers' and fathers' perceptions of child deviance: roles of parent and child behaviors and parent adjustment. *Journal of Consulting and Clinical Psychology* 56: 909–915.

Wertsch, J. V. & J. Youniss. (1987). Contextualizing the investigator: The case of developmental psychology. *Human Development* 30: 18–31.

Wuthnow, R. (1989). *Communities of discourse*. Cambridge, MA: Cambridge University Press.

Yogman, M. W., D. Kindlon, & F. Earls. (1995). Father involvement and cognitive/behavioral outcomes of preterm infants. *Journal of the American Academy of Child and Adolescent Psychiatry* 34(1): 58–66.

Youniss, J. (1975). Another perspective on social cognition. In A. Pick. Ed. *Minnesota Symposium on Child Psychology*. Vol. 9, 173–193. Minneapolis, MN: University of Minnesota Press.

Zigler, E. & S. J. Styfco. (1993). Using research and theory to justify and inform Head Start expansion. *Social Policy Report Society for Research in Child Development* 7(2): 1–20.

Zill, N., G. Resnick, & R. McKey. (2000). *What children know and can do at the end of Head Start and what it tells us about the program's performance*. Washington, DC: Department of Health and Human Services. Advisory Committee on Head Start Research and Evaluation. Retrieved from www2. acf.dhhs.gov/programs/hsb/hsreac/faces.

Zimmerman, S. L. (1999). Family policy research: A systems view. *Family Science Review* 12(2): 113–130.